Summarization
in Any Subject

50 Techniques to Improve Student Learning

Rick Wormeli

ASCD

ASCD®

1703 N. Beauregard St. • Alexandria, VA 22311-1714 USA
Phone: 800-933-2723 or 703-578-9600 • Fax: 703-575-5400
Web site: www.ascd.org • E-mail: member@ascd.org
Author guidelines: www.ascd.org/write

Gene R. Carter, *Executive Director*; Nancy Modrak, *Director of Publishing*; Julie Houtz, *Director of Book Editing & Production*; Katie Martin, *Project Manager*; Shelley Kirby, *Senior Graphic Designer*; Mary Ann Paniccia, *Typesetter*; Vivian Coss, *Production Specialist*

Printed in the United States of America. Cover art copyright © 2005 by ASCD. ASCD publications present a variety of viewpoints. The views expressed or implied in this book should not be interpreted as official positions of the Association.

Paperback ISBN-13: 978-1-4166-0019-0 • Paperback ISBN-10: 1-4166-0019-1
ASCD product #104014   s12/04

Also available as an e-book through ebrary, netLibrary, and many online book sellers (see Books in Print for the ISBNs).

Quantity discounts for the paperback book: 10–49 copies, 10%; 50–499 copies, 15%; for 500 or more copies, call 800-933-2723, ext. 5634, or 703-575-5634.

Library of Congress Cataloging-in-Publication Data
Wormeli, Rick.
    Summarization in any subject : 50 techniques to improve student learning / Rick Wormeli.
       p. cm.
Includes bibliographical references and index.
    ISBN 1-4166-0019-1 (alk. paper)
    1. Communication in education. 2. Abstracting. 3. Cognitive learning. I. Title.

    LB1033.5.W67 2005
    371.39—dc22

                                                     2004021200

15   14   13   12   11   10

Summarization
in Any Subject

●● **Acknowledgments** v

●● **1 The Case for Summarization** 1

●● **2 Summarization Savvy** 7

●● **3 Summarization Techniques** 31

3–2–1 39

Acronyms 41

Advance Organizers 44

Analysis Matrices and Graphic Organizers.............. 46

Backwards Summaries.. 57

Bloom's Taxonomy Summary Cubes 60

Body Analogies... 64

Body Sculpture 68

Build a Model... 73

Camp Songs 78

Carousel Brainstorming 81

Charades.. 83

Concrete Spellings 85

Design a Test 87

Exclusion Brainstorming 89

The Frayer Model 91

Human Bingo.. 94

Human Continuum 97

Inner or Outer Circle 102

Jigsaws 104

Learning Logs and Journals 106

Lineup 108

Luck of the Draw 113

Moving Summarizations 114

Multiple Intelligences 118

One-Word Summaries 122

P-M-I 124

Partners A and B 127

Point of View 129

P-Q-R-S-T 131

RAFT 133

Save the Last Word for Me 136

Share One; Get One 138

Socratic Seminars 140

Something-Happened-and-Then/Somebody-Wanted-But-So 146

Sorting Cards 149

Spelling Bee de Strange 151

SQ3R 153

Summarization Pyramids 155

Summary Ball 158

Synectic Summaries 160

T-Chart/T-List 164

Taboo® 167

Test Notes 170

Think-Pair-Share 172

Traditional Rules-Based Summaries 174

Triads 177

Unique Summarization Assignments 180

Verbs? Change Them! 185

Word Splash 188

Conclusion 191

●● **Appendix: Sample Texts and
Summarization Practice Activities** 193

Resources 219

Index 221

About the Author 226

Acknowledgments

Special thanks to my colleagues who are English and reading teachers and to writer mentors who, through multiple discussions in person and by e-mail, helped me carve a vision for this book. I'd also like to thank my students, who put up with our many experiments in summary writing, either knowingly or not.

I am indebted to those writers and speakers who make cognitive theory accessible and compelling to teachers who don't often have the time to do the research necessary to keep up with all we're discovering about how humans learn. The following individuals inspire hope and give us the tools to teach: Thomas Armstrong, Glenda Ward Beamon, John D. Bransford, John T. Bruer, Renate and Geoffrey Caine, Bruce Campbell, Art Costa, Marian Diamond, Robin Fogarty, Howard Gardner, Jim Grant, Pierce J. Howard, David Hyerle, Eric Jensen, Robert Marzano, Carol O'Connor, Steven Pinker, Joseph Renzulli, Lynda Rice, Spence Rogers, Debbie Silver, David Sousa, Marilee Sprenger, Barbara Strauch, Robert Sylwester, Carol Ann Tomlinson, and Pat Wolfe.

Thanks to Monte Selby—husband, dad, educator, musician, coach, and catalyst—for elevating the importance of literacy and cognitive practices in the university crowd.

As always, my greatest thanks go to my wife, Kelly, and children, Ryan and Lynn, who show me what's important in life every day.

Part 1

The Case for Summarization

"AS YOU READ THIS BOOK, PLEASE STOP AT REGULAR INTERVALS AND SUMMARIZE WHAT YOU'VE READ."

For some readers, such a task is sensible, even enjoyable. They know a variety of summarization techniques, and they've experienced the illumination that comes from successfully summarizing material.

The rest of us may wonder if all that work is necessary. Isn't it enough just to read the book? We have a lot of pages to get through and that great idea we're looking for may be coming up soon. Besides, we have so much else to do too. The dishes stacked in the sink aren't going to wash themselves.

Most teachers will agree that our students are usually of the latter disposition—meaning they're ready to do anything except summarize. Copying a page from the dictionary is preferable to summarizing a page in their history book. What's important and what's not, they wonder. What if they don't get it all? What if they include too much? What's the main idea of this paragraph? What are the supporting details? How do they (and why *should* they) restate the sentence in a new way when the author has already said it as clearly as anyone can? A lack of clarity and specific methods can give any instructional strategy a bad reputation; with summarization, they can be deal breakers.

First, what is summarization? It is restating the essence of text or an experience in as few words as possible or in a new, yet efficient, manner. Many students and teachers assume that summarization must be done in writing—either with a pencil and paper or on a keyboard. This assumption misses summarization's great dexterity. Yes, it can be done in writing, but also orally, dramatically, artistically, visually, physically, musically, in groups, or individually. Summarization is one of the most underused teaching techniques we have today, yet research has shown that it yields some of the greatest leaps in comprehension and long-term retention of information.

Robert Marzano, Debra Pickering, and Jane Pollock (2001) cite extensive research studies in their book, *Classroom Instruction That Works: Research-Based Strategies for Increasing Student Achievement*, to prove summarization is among the top nine most effective teaching strategies in the history of education. Specifically, pages 29–48 on summarizing and note-taking; pages 72–83 on nonlinguistic representations; and pages 111–120 on cues, questions, and advanced organizers provide ample evidence of the learning power of summarizing and the advantages of actively processing information, rather than just receiving it passively. This book and the accompanying *A Handbook for Classroom Instruction That Works* (2002) are highly recommended, both as a rationale for summarizing and as a source of tips on how to do it well.

Some readers are aware of the evidence that cognitive theory provides to support the pedagogical power of summarization. One element of cognitive theory that seems particularly consistent with summarization is the primacy–recency effect (Sousa, 2003) or, as some refer to it, Prime 1 and Prime 2. The primacy–recency effect says that we remember best what we experience first in a lesson, and we remember second best what we experience last. A good teacher, then, exposes students to most of the big truths of each lesson within the first 10 minutes or so of the class and then reviews those truths again at the end. This approach makes sense. Think about how our own teachers taught us to make persuasive speeches: put the strongest evidence for our argument at the beginning, they said, and repeat that evidence at the end. Because people wouldn't remember the middle portion as well, that was the place for less-than-powerful information.

By structuring lessons to embrace the primacy–recency effect, we teachers can change what our students will remember. For example, if Mario's teacher begins a lesson with management and clerical tasks, such as checking homework, taking attendance, making announcements, and collecting permission slips, students will move the information associated with those tasks into their long-term memory. So when Mom asks, "What did you learn in school today?" Mario will respond, "Sheila was absent, I missed six of the math problems, and Friday is Funny Hat Day. Hey, Mom, does Dad have a funny hat I can wear?"

If Mario's teacher had structured the class around primacy–recency, thus exposing students to the big concepts of the day during the first 10 minutes, Mario would have responded a little differently to his mom's inquiry: "We learned how to figure out the surface area of a cylinder. You find the area of the top circle, then multiply it by two, next find the area of the rectangle that wraps around the middle, and, finally, add its area to the circle's area." This response might sound like a teacher's fantasy, but the technique really works. When you hit the key concepts first and last thing in your lessons, those ideas are what students will retain. The clerical and management peripherals won't get in the way.

That last portion of class is critical. Ideally, this time should be set aside for reflection and summarization. Little learning occurs as a result of instruction alone. The kind of true learning that lasts will occur only if we apply newly acquired concepts outside of the initial learning experience, and if we spend time reflecting on and processing what we've learned. That expanded knowledge is what summarization is all about.

From an instructional standpoint, this step takes conviction. You must be willing to stop your lesson early and summarize, even if you haven't taught your final point. To summon the courage to do this, ask yourself, "Am I teaching so that students will learn, or am I teaching so that I can cover the required material?" If you truly care about what students take with them at the end of the school year, then it's easier to choose summarization and reflection activities over coverage. Think about it: *covering* something can also mean "removing it from view." What teacher wants to conceal the Bill of Rights, the body's metabolism, literary devices, chemical equations, and geometry from students? Unfortunately, when you don't provide students with the time they need to reflect on such topics and to reach and apply new understandings, you limit their learning.

In a typical school week, can you summarize every lesson every day? No. Life gets in the way. Fire drills, assemblies, extended class discussions, surprise visits from parents or administrators, computer crashes, and 50 other interruptions can occur. Nonetheless, you should always have summarization as a goal. If you and your students get in three good summarization activities between Monday and Friday, you've had a good week.

There used to be a television commercial about orange juice with the tag line, "Orange juice: It's not just for breakfast any more." The same can be said of summarization. Even though it's a good way to end a lesson, it's not *just* for the end of lessons. Use summarization structures to pre-assess students before teaching them; then use students' responses to inform and change your instruction. Use summarization techniques in the midst of a unit to help students monitor their own comprehension and to generate feedback for you on how their comprehension is developing. And, of course, use summarization after a learning experience so students can process or make sense of what has been learned and can move the material into long-term memory.

Lecturing is one place teachers can see the power of frequent summarization. Although lecturing is a common practice, particularly in high school, research tells us that information students take in via a typical, 45-minute lecture is not likely to make it to long-term memory (Sousa, 2001b). In contrast, lectures that are delivered in "chunks," instead of one long whole, result in a tremendous amount of information moving to long-term memory. Chunking a lecture means the teacher speaks for approximately 15 minutes (6 to 7 minutes in the primary grades), then pauses and facilitates a summarizing or processing experience about the information just presented. Such summarizations can last from 1 to 10 minutes, as necessary. Then the teacher continues the lecture.

One reason a chunked lecture works for information retention is because it "psychs out" the brain, making it feel as if it's no longer at the saturation point. It has room to contemplate more because it has placed the recent material into a metaphorical file for safekeeping and future retrieval. Leaving the summarization for the end of our 45-minute or longer lecture does not result in the same amount of mastery as smaller summaries throughout the class. We summarize en route to mastery.

Another place in which we can see summarization's power is a "Ropes Initiatives" or "Project Adventure" course. Anyone who has navigated 12-foot walls, whipped down zip wires in harnesses, or passed through openings in a roped "spider web" without ringing the attached bell knows that real learning doesn't occur while you are doing the thing itself. Learning comes in the debriefing afterward, when the instructor helps the members of the group process what they have accomplished: How did you solve the problem? What hindered the group's arriving at a workable solution? How did Jennifer's suggestion add to Karen's? What would you do differently next time? What does this activity teach us about teamwork?

You might begin to explain the value of summarization to your students by talking about one of its clear applications: writing news articles. Relating what has been observed or experienced in a clear, succinct manner for a particular audience is a helpful skill to master. Furthermore, in almost all of today's high tech companies, employees must be able to read or perceive something, then make sense of it by manipulating the information, regrouping it, and applying it to a new situation. That process is similar to the one reporters use to relate the news. Summarization is a real-world skill.

Students today must learn facts, of course, but they must also be skilled "information archeologists." They must dig for information, make sense of it, and attach meaning to it. They're charged with getting the main ideas as well as their supportive details, the principle arguments as well as their evidence. One of the greatest gifts we can give to students, then, is to teach them (1) how to identify salient information, no matter what subject we teach or how we present it, and (2) how to structure that information for meaning and successful application. Summarizing is a learned process of deleting, substituting, and keeping information (Marzano et al., 2001). The trick is to see summarization beyond "a nice idea if we had time to use it" . . . or another ineffective add-on for an already bursting curriculum . . . or something associated with writing that we don't want to impose on our students or on our limited grading energy.

We shouldn't tell students to summarize information just so they will be able to retell it; there's no point to "just retelling," and our students are not parrots-in-training. We should teach students to summarize with the awareness that it is a strategy that will open a topic for their minds and will make the content stick. It leads students to the comprehension and retention that is the goal of learning, the goal of every teacher. In Parts 2 and 3, we'll explore how easy, varied, and effective summarizing can be.

Part 2

Summarization Savvy

SUMMARIZING IS NOT AN INNATE SKILL THAT ONLY A FEW PEOPLE HAVE. Nor is it anything magical; Harry Potter can summarize his potions text without using his wand. The big secrets of how to summarize are not secrets at all: Students must be tenacious, must learn multiple methods of summarizing, must practice, and must be inclined to revise their thinking as perspective and information warrant.

Let's begin by looking at original text from a history book and then at its summarization:

From *A History of US, Vol. 10: All The People: 1945–2001* by Joy Hakim. Copyright © 1995 by Joy Hakim. Used by permission of Oxford University Press, Inc.

ORIGINAL TEXT: *The Sea Around Us* made Rachel Carson famous; the last book she wrote, *Silent Spring*, brought her enemies (among some powerful interest groups). It took courage to write that book. It was a look at a grim subject—pesticides—and how they were poisoning the earth and its inhabitants. In *Silent Spring*, Carson attacked the chemical and food-processing industries, and the Department of Agriculture.

They lost no time in fighting back. Rachel Carson was mocked and ridiculed as a 'hysterical woman.' Her editor wrote, "Her opponents must have realized . . . that she was questioning not only the indiscriminate use of poisons but [also] the basic irresponsibility of an industrialized, technological society toward the natural world."

But the fury and fervor of the attacks only brought her more readers. President [John F.] Kennedy asked for a special report on pesticides from his Science Advisory Committee. The report confirmed what Carson had written, and it made important recommendations for curtailing and controlling the use of pesticides.

The public, which had been generally unaware of the danger of the poisons sprayed on plants, was now aware. Modestly, Rachel Carson said that one book couldn't change things but on that she may have been wrong.

SUMMARY: When it was published, Rachel Carson's *Silent Spring* angered many people. The book opened the public's eyes to the devastating use of pesticides on animals and plants, and it attacked companies that used them callously. The companies ridiculed Carson and her work, but the government investigated her claims and found they were true. The government responded to the danger by regulating pesticide use.

This is an effective summary, but what makes it effective? How did the summarizer know which portions to underline and bring together to form the summary? The answer is summarization savvy, and there are specific practices teachers can use to help our students acquire it, increasing their summarizing success and enhancing their understanding in all subject areas. Let's examine a few of those strategies now.

Activate Students' Personal Background Knowledge

Each student's background and experience with a topic will shape the summary he creates. For example, if you ask a student who's passionate about baseball and a student who has never played or watched baseball to summarize the life of a famous baseball player, you'll receive two very different summaries. As another example, some southerners call the U.S. Civil War "the War of Northern Aggression." The connotations that come with that perspective will color what students pick up when reading about that period of U.S. history.

Imagine the different viewpoints of these three people who are reading Michael Crichton's *Jurassic Park*: a theologian, an expert on Chaos Theory, and an office clerk looking to read a spirited adventure while on vacation. Each brings different expectations to the book, and each takes away something significantly different, too; their varied experiences weave particular kinds of filters for the content. Good teachers recognize that background knowledge influences learning outcomes, and they capitalize on it.

To enable students to pick out the important elements we want them to take away from text, or from any learning experience, we must make sure they begin with enough background to gather those intended understandings. In some situations, this may mean creating a background where there was none—a process that might require a whole class period or two. For example, before I have my science students read and summarize an article about how microscopes work, I set aside time for them to play with actual microscopes: adjusting the light source and the various objectives, clamping slides to the stage, and focusing the lens on what's under the coverslip. Afterward, when they read the technical passage on microscopes, they don't exhibit a glazed-eye look. Everything they read moves into long-term memory—which is the goal—because the passage is attached to their earlier microscope experience already in storage. That knowledge gives meaning to the text. Because very little goes into long-term memory unless it's attached to something already there, teachers must create an initial foundation to which students can attach new learning. Socrates was right: "All thinking begins with wonder." We can't afford to leave wonder to chance.

Prime the Students' Brains

In *Brain Matters* (2001), Pat Wolfe writes that the human brain needs to be primed so it can pay attention and determine what's meaningful in any text or experience. For example, we waste time if we just ask students to read Chapter 17 of their history textbook and to determine what's important enough to summarize. It would be the same as asking them to watch a 50-minute video on solar systems with no direction beyond "Take notes." They might write down everything or nothing, but either way, very little of the information would go into long-term memory. Conversely, if we ask students to "watch this video and focus on how planets maintain their orbits in a solar system," then we're giving them a target—something specific they can pay attention to. With this priming, the students will be able to do something with the information in the video, increasing the likelihood that it will take up permanent residence in memory.

To show the importance of priming students' brains before they read and summarize, ask your students to read an esoteric passage on something about which they have little familiarity and write a summary afterward. Don't set a purpose for their reading, and don't provide any background. Then ask them to do the same task with another article of similar difficulty, but this time, give them a specific focus and background on the topic. When they have finished, have them compare the quality of the two summaries, which will be markedly different. For further evidence, give your students a quiz on the material after each experience. The scores will be better on the material for which they were given purpose prior to reading. I highly recommend Cris Tovani's *I Read It, But I Don't Get It* (2000), which has an excellent discussion of priming the brain and providing background knowledge.

Teach Students to Identify a Text's Underlying Structure

In my experience, students understand—and summarize—best those text structures with which they are most familiar. It's important, then, for teachers in every subject area to teach their students about the various ways authors structure text and about the various graphic formats they can use to summarize that text effectively. For example, if your students are reading an article about two systems of government, you want them to be able to pick up on the text's compare-and-contrast structure and know that a good way to summarize the article's information would be to use a Venn diagram—two interlocking circles, with the unique characteristics for each government system recorded in the outer portions of the individual circles and common characteristics of the two systems recorded in the area that the circles overlap. If the article is comparing four types of government (or more), you want them to know that a matrix structure, with the names the systems of government arranged along the vertical axis and attributes of those systems along the horizontal axis, would be an effective way of summarizing the information.

Most written text is presented in one of the following structures, or in a combination of two or more: enumeration, chronological order, compare and contrast, cause and effect, or problem and solution. Here's a closer look at each, accompanied by examples. You can find additional illustrations of the suggested summary structures throughout this book.

Enumeration

Enumeration focuses on listing facts, characteristics, features, or a combination of those. Signal words include these: *to begin with, first, second, third, then, next, finally, several, numerous, for example, for instance, in fact, most important, also,* and *in addition.*

ORIGINAL TEXT: The moon is our closest neighbor. It's 250,000 miles away. Its gravity is only one-sixth that of Earth. Thus, a boy weighing 120 pounds in Virginia would weigh only 20 pounds on the moon. In addition, there is no atmosphere on the moon. The footprints left by astronauts back in 1969 are still there, as crisply formed as they were on the day they were made. The lack of atmosphere also means there is no water on the moon, an important problem when traveling there.

Suggested summarization formats for enumeration structures include mind maps; webs (wheel-and-spoke outline); vertical outlines; concentric circles; Cornell notes; matrices; The Frayer Model; word sorts and other categorizing/classifying structures; main idea with supporting detail sections; and staircase organizers, with major points on each step and connections to other ideas written on the vertical risers and railings.

Here's an example:

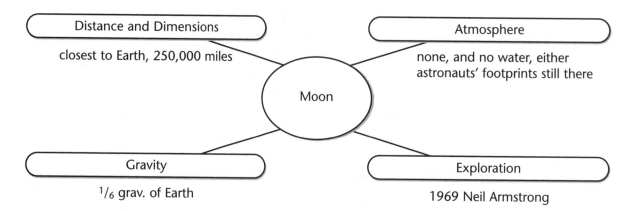

Distance and Dimensions
closest to Earth, 250,000 miles

Atmosphere
none, and no water, either
astronauts' footprints still there

Moon

Gravity
$1/6$ grav. of Earth

Exploration
1969 Neil Armstrong

Chronological Order

Chronological, or time, order refers to structures that put facts, events, and concepts into sequence using time references. Signal words include these: *after, before, gradually, not long after, now, on* (date)*, since, when,* and *while.*

ORIGINAL TEXT: Astronomy came a long way in the 1500s and 1600s. In 1531, what we now know as Halley's Comet made an appearance and caused great panic. Just 12 years later, Copernicus realized that the sun, not Earth, was the center of the solar system, and astronomy became a way to understand the natural world, not something to fear. In the early part of the next century, Galileo made the first observations with a new instrument—the telescope. A generation later, Sir Isaac Newton invented the reflecting telescope, a close cousin to what we use today. Halley's Comet returned in 1682 and it was treated as a scientific wonder, studied by Edmund Halley.

Suggested summarization formats for chronological structures include time lines, flow charts, mind maps, calendars, and clock faces. Here's an example:

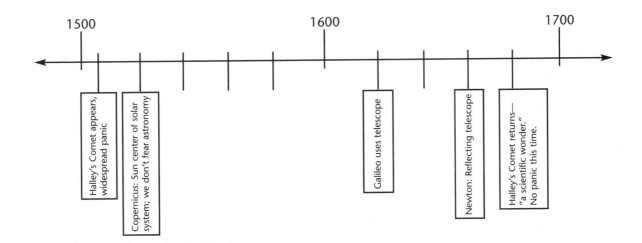

Compare and Contrast

Compare-and-contrast structures explain similarities and differences. Signal words include *although, as well as, but, conversely, either, however, not only, on the one hand, on the other hand, or, rather than, similarly, unless,* and *unlike.*

ORIGINAL TEXT: Middle school gives students more autonomy than elementary school. While students are asked to be responsible for their learning in both levels, middle school students have more pressure to complete assignments on their own rather than rely on adults. In addition, narrative forms are used to teach most literacy skills in elementary school. [But] expository writing is the way most information is given in middle school.

Suggested summarization formats for compare-and-contrast structures include Venn diagrams, T-charts, similarities/differences flow charts, matrices, The Frayer Model, and double-bubble maps. Here's an example:

	Student autonomy	Student responsibility for learning	Student completes most assignments...	Writing type most used to teach literacy
Middle school	high	high	on own	expository
Elementary school	low	low	with teacher or parent help	narrative

Cause and Effect

Cause-and-effect structures show how something can happen as a result of something else having happened. Signal words include *accordingly, as a result, because, consequently, nevertheless, so that, therefore, this led to,* and *thus.*

ORIGINAL TEXT: Drug abusers often start in upper elementary school. They experiment with a parent's beer and hard liquor, enjoying the buzz they receive. They keep doing this, and it starts taking more and more of the alcohol to get the same level of buzz. As a result, the child turns to other forms of stimulation, including marijuana. These steps can lead to more hardcore drugs, such as angel dust (PCP), heroin, and crack cocaine; consequently, marijuana and alcohol are known as "gateway drugs." Because of their addictive nature, these gateway drugs lead many youngsters who use them into the world of hardcore drugs.

Suggested summarization formats for cause-and-effect structures include flow charts; webs; "herringbones"; cluster graphics; wheel-and-spoke outlines; and trait analyses. Here's an example:

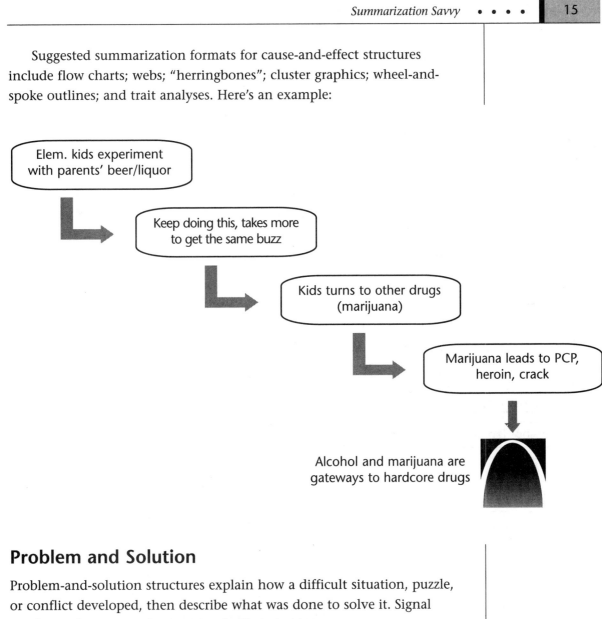

Problem and Solution

Problem-and-solution structures explain how a difficult situation, puzzle, or conflict developed, then describe what was done to solve it. Signal words are the same as for cause-and-effect structures.

ORIGINAL TEXT: The carrying capacity of a habitat refers to the amount of plant and animal life its resources can hold. For example, if there are only 80 pounds of food available and there are animals that together need more than 80 pounds of food to survive, one or more animals will die—the habitat can't "carry" them. Humans have reduced many habitats' carrying capacity by imposing limiting factors that reduce that capacity. Limiting factors include housing developments, road construction, dams, pollution, fires, and acid rain. So that forest habitats can maintain full carrying capacities, Congress has enacted legislation that protects endangered habitats from human development or impact. As a result, these areas have high carrying capacities and an abundance of plant and animal life.

Suggested summarization formats for problem-solution structures also mirror those for cause-and-effect structures: flow charts, webs, "herring-bones," cluster graphics, wheel-and-spoke outlines, and trait analyses. Here's an example:

Factors That Limit a Habitat's Carrying Capacity

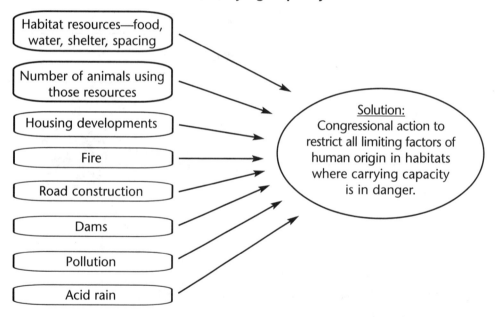

Teach Students to Follow Clues to Meaning

Most students in the upper grades will be familiar with the most common and effective kinds of writing, such as expository writing and persuasive writing. However, it's important to make sure students get a sense of general expository and persuasive structures. For example, expository writing often begins with an introduction, moves to several paragraphs of explanation, and then ends with a one-paragraph conclusion. A persuasive piece, such as a political speech or a newspaper editorial, generally puts its strongest arguments in the beginning and the end, not in the middle. Although these are simple structures, they can elude many students, and it's worth stressing them repeatedly in your classes.

One valuable clue to meaning is a topic sentence. A topic sentence refers to the topic of the paragraph or section of text and the claim that the author makes about it. For example, in the sentence "Dogs are great pets," "dogs" is the topic and "are great pets" is the claim made about it. Of course, the topic sentence of a paragraph may not always be so clearly stated, and it may be in the middle or end of a paragraph, not just at the beginning. And sometimes, a topic sentence is just implied—it's up to the reader to tease it out by combining fragments of several sentences. I recommend giving students repeated practice in determining the topic sentences of various paragraphs. (See the Appendix for sample text and a practice activity.)

Why stress these structures? Knowing how text is put together helps students know where to look to find the key information. For example, the paragraphs that construct persuasive pieces will contain clues to the elements of the argument. To help your students find what's important in a piece of text, teach them to begin their search within specific paragraphs. For instance, the first and last sentences of a paragraph are often full of clues as to what's important in that paragraph. Any boldfaced or italicized words are additional clues and always worth investigating. Text size and a change in the font are also indicators of importance, particularly in advertising copy or written directions. Information pulled from the text and set-off with a border or shading usually signals something worth remembering. Finally, teaching your students some of the signal words just mentioned can orient them further to both the logic of the text and the importance of each piece of information it contains.

As anyone who's taken a college literature course in the past 35 years will attest, a "text" does not have to be a written document. Be sure to teach students to follow clues to meaning that are present in nonwritten text situations, as well. For example, point out how lecturers often forecast their arguments with statements like, "Here are the three points I want to make," and underscore the most important things they've talked about (and the most important things for anyone taking notes on the lecture to write down) with phrases like, "In conclusion . . ." Mention that audio texts frequently incorporate repetition to continually point to what's important and keep the listener engaged. Remind students of the latest politician's often-repeated tag line or an annoying commercial jingle to help them grasp the power that repetition has to focus a listener's attention.

It is also important to address clues to meaning within "visual texts" like photographs, movies, Web sites, magazine layouts, and advertisements. When we look at photographs, we might consider the framing of the scene in the photo, what's left out of the frame, the balance of color or objects in the photo, the shading, the lighting, what's in focus, and what's out of focus, in order to "read" what the photographer considered salient. Teach students to note how movies are edited and framed, how perspectives are chosen and not chosen, what scenes are shown and not shown, and how the music helps to evoke a mood or foreshadow what's to come.

Finally, it's helpful to guide students through multiple experiences in which they analyze nonwritten text-media in terms of the designer's intent and how he or she has elevated the important elements so that they would really stick with the viewer. Push these kinds of questions: What are the important aspects of the museum display and how do we know they are the important aspects? How do we know what's important on this food can label, and is what we consider important the same thing that the manufacturer thinks is important? What is the salient information to be gleaned from this television commercial, and how did the producers of the commercial make that information salient for the viewer? When we look at a Web site, how do we know what to elevate in importance and what to allow to fade into the visual background? With a little practice, students get very good at following these sorts of clues to meaning, enhancing their analytical ability and their media savvy. Lynell Burmark's wonderful book *Visual Literacy* (2001) is an excellent source of practical approaches to this topic.

Introduce Students to Analogies

Analogies are extremely useful when summarizing, which is why it's important to explain and model the concept. I once taught students about the unscrupulous Boss Tweed of Tammany Hall in New York City during the mid-1800s. When it came time for them to process the information, I asked groups to make analogies between what we learned about Boss Tweed and parts of the human body (minus the genitalia, for obvious reasons). After an extended discussion, one group presented a drawing of a stick-figure human with an arrow pointing to a Valentine-shaped heart drawn in the center of the figure's torso. A paragraph next to the arrow explained how Boss Tweed was like the human heart. I confess that the clash between traditional associations of the heart as a source of love, caring, and nurture and the awful corruption of Boss Tweed made me respond prematurely.

"Come on," I told the students. "The heart? How can you back that up? He was the opposite of what the heart is normally considered to influence."

One of the students confronted me. "Wait a minute, Mr. Wormeli. Boss Tweed donated some of his money to charities. That made him look good in the public's eye, and he needed to manipulate the masses from time to time. It was still a good deed. The heart is associated with caring acts."

"Yes, but that's one small side of Boss Tweed," I interjected. "What about all his other acts? What about—?"

One student flashed his open palm in the air to stop me. "Wait. We're not done," he said. "Boss Tweed gave the city money to help it through tough times. He always got something out of it, but he kept departments going when there was trouble. He pumped money and influence into the city to give it life. Isn't that what the human heart does for the human body—pump blood throughout the body to give it life?"

All eyes shot from the student to me for a counterpoint.

I was silent a moment before breaking into a smile. What a sorry world this would be if my students were limited to my creativity. "Touché," I said. "You did it. You saw more than one side. I couldn't have done it."

With each group's example, we discussed whether or not the analogy was accurate and complete. We even pursued other correlations as we compared Boss Tweed and the human body. In the end, the discussion was more important than the final drawing and written analogies. In each analogy, we isolated critical attributes and argued the merits of various symbolic representations of those attributes. The complex process resulted in students retaining more long-term information than they would have in most other assignments. I'm glad I didn't settle for "Describe Boss Tweed," or "Answer the four comprehension questions at the end of the textbook chapter."

Chunk Text and Learning Experiences

Long text passages can be daunting to someone learning to summarize. A student's brain will more effectively process information that is "chunked" into shorter segments for a summary en route to understanding the full passage. Breaking text into segments does not dilute its message; rather, it presents the message in a way that enhances student learning. When students encounter information in these smaller segments, more of it goes into their long-term memories. Consider breaking learning experiences, lectures, and readings into shorter segments before asking your students to summarize them. As an authority on both the content you're teaching and about how your students learn best, you can preview your curriculum (a section of text, a particular concept you'll be demonstrating, a topic you'll be discussing) and determine the best way to present it to your students.

Here's an example. On page 195 in the Appendix, you'll find the Gettysburg Address. If I were to just hand a group of students this whole speech and ask them to make sense of it, the odds that all the students would come away understanding it would be pretty long. Those odds would improve exponentially if I took some time to "unpack" it with them. Assuming that I've already provided historical context, defined difficult vocabulary, and read through it aloud once so students can hear voice inflections to aid comprehension, the next step to successful student learning is to "chunk" the speech into meaningful segments. There are lots of ways I might group larger sections into shorter sections, but one helpful way is focus on those transition words:

> Four score and seven years ago our fathers brought forth on this continent, a new nation, conceived in Liberty, and dedicated to the proposition that all men are created equal.

> Now we are engaged in a great civil war, testing whether that nation, or any nation so conceived and so dedicated, can long endure. We are met on a great battle-field of that war.

Does anything here suggest a natural shift in the content? Yes.
Lincoln begins by alluding to the past ("ago"), but then he starts the second paragraph with the word "Now." This creates a time line of sorts, contrasting where we were with where we are today (in his time). So, I might chunk the first section according to time period referenced.

Depending on my students' readiness, I could also simplify things by first offering this cut-out-the-fat version of the first sentence:

"Four score and seven years ago, our fathers brought forth a new nation dedicated to the proposition that all men are created equal."

Once I'm sure everyone has grasped the meaning of these words, I would add Lincoln's clarifying phrases, "on this continent" and "conceived in Liberty" in their proper places, discussing with students why Lincoln added them.

As an alternative, I might chunk this presentation by asking students to focus on one or two essential questions, such as, "What was Lincoln's purpose for the speech?" and "Did he succeed?" Examination of the text reveals several clues to Lincoln's intent, such as, "We have come to dedicate," and, "we take increased devotion to that cause for which they gave the last full measure of devotion—that we here highly resolve these dead shall not have died in vain."

When first teaching students something experiential, we focus on practicing new behaviors in short chunks. When teaching students to write in cursive, for instance, we ask them to practice specific strokes that are subsets of the more complicated ones they'll do later, when they write capital letters. In band or orchestra, we sometimes ask students to practice a measure or two over and over until playing those measures is almost automatic, then we ask students to practice the transition into those measures until the transitions are smooth, as well. We're able to set up these focus segments best if we've considered ways to chunk experiences ahead of teaching them to students, of course, but there are times when inspiration hits, and we chunk things differently right on the spot. Embrace those moments; they may be some of your best moments as a teacher.

In short, chunking text or experiences requires teachers to look at the bottom line of what we want students to learn—the essential and enduring aspects we are trying to teach. When it's helpful, we diagram the text or experience ourselves prior to teaching, and we play with the structures a little to see which ones increase the likelihood of students learning the material. The more we do it, the easier it gets. Of course, if the material is new to us, we can still do a good job presenting it in chunks; this is a great time to try out a presentation with a mentor or colleague and ask for a critique.

Give Students Tools for Encountering Text

Before students can summarize a piece of writing, they have to know what's in it. In order to know what's in it, they have to be conscious of it. This sounds obvious, but a surprising number of students read a passage of text and have no awareness of what they read. They don't engage with the text in any way; they simply pass their eyes across the words. I compare it to the way we sometimes zone out when driving long distances, suddenly realizing that we don't recall anything about the last 20 minutes of our trip. Gosh, we think, I hope I didn't miss my turn. Teaching students how to approach text mindfully—and giving them the tools they need to do so—is essential to promoting summarization savvy.

Repeated Reading

Good summarizers read text passages at least twice: once to get the general overview and then again to determine what is salient. In our fast-paced world, convincing students to take the time to read passages twice may be difficult, but the practice will be among the more mature attributes they gain. Stress to students that as readers, we can determine what is important only when we have a general view of what's coming. As we decipher each sentence, we use the lines that precede and succeed that sentence. We can't do that in the first read-through, because we only have access to the preceding sentence and the current one. The second time through, we have a better idea of our purpose for reading.

Making Notations and Marking Text

Once we know why we're reading, we need to make the notes that will help us interact with the text and speak and write about it intelligently.

Students often read something but still don't know what to think about it. Reading notations are a way of breaking text into smaller pieces, making it easy to gather essential details and construct a response. They are well worth teaching, modeling, and using.

When it comes to the notations themselves, you and your students should feel free to make up your own symbols. For someone just getting started, I recommend the following:

✓ I agree with this.
X I disagree with this.
?? I'm confused by this.
!! Wow! (It elicits a strong emotion.)
CL The statement is a general claim.
EV Here is evidence for the claim (these symbols can be numbered to indicate their sequence too: EV1, EV2, EV3, and so forth).

Notice that the first two aren't "I understand this" and "I don't understand this." Asking students to agree or disagree with something requires them to take a stance, something that they must back up with evidence or a rationale. They must make a personal investment in the meaning; thus, they must internalize the concept.

If students are not allowed to write or mark in books and materials, they can use sticky pads (such as Post-it® notes), highlighting tape, or acetate (transparency) overlays. Multicolored sticky pads come in varied sizes and are great for marking notations and identifying excerpts for later reference. Teach students to use them effectively.

Another option is highlighting tape, a very thin, vinyl-like, reusable tape that students can use to underline sentences, to frame paragraphs, or to place vertically along a passage to mark it for future reference. The tape lays flat on the page, so students can close their books without affecting the book's binding. It comes in different colors that can be used to mark different text attributes. The tape peels off the book page with no damage to the page or print and can be reused. You can find highlighting tape in some office supply stores or can order rolls from the educational book publisher, Crystal Springs Books, for reasonable prices.

When asking students to write on transparencies at the overhead projector, such as for solving math problems, editing a paragraph, or drawing a diagram, remember to clip a blank transparency on top of your master transparency. Students will then write on the blank transparency but will appear to be writing on the master. When they finish, you can replace the used transparency with a clean one.

After students have read the text and made notations in light pencil or on Post-it® notes, they're ready to summarize because they have a handle on the content. In class discussions, momentum isn't stopped by students scanning line by line the section they didn't understand. They simply look for the question mark symbol and instantly see what they wanted to ask the teacher. If a teacher requests the author's evidence for a stated claim, students can look for the "EV" notation. As they process data in a graph or a particular summarization structure, students can focus directly on the author's essential arguments and supporting details.

Students also may find it helpful to draw concepts that they read or experience, rather than write, highlight, or underline them. These often become semi-collages of ideas but there is a flow to the drawings that the summarizer retains when he explains the drawings to others. That last step is important—students explaining the artistic portrayal to others. Create opportunities where they can do this.

Stress Scholarly Objectivity

Students should understand that a summary is a clear and undistorted distillation of a reading, lecture, or experience. Summaries are about the author's arguments and details; they are not the place for personal opinions or judgments. If students need support in this area, teach them to preface their written and spoken summaries with the phrase, "According to the author [or speaker, or experience leader]." This technique helps to keep them focused on what was truly in the text or experience and reminds them to form their interpretations and reactions separately. It's an analytical practice that serves all scholars well.

Teach Students to Evaluate Their Summaries

Creating the initial summary is just the first step in the summarization process. Teach students to evaluate each rough draft summary with questions like these:

- Does it convey the information accurately?

- Is it too narrow or too broad? Does it convey all of the important elements? Does it convey too much?

- Would someone else using this summary gain all he or she needed to know to understand the subject?

- Are the ideas in the right sequence?

- Did I leave out my opinion and just report an undistorted essence of the original content?

- Did I use my own words and style?

Stress to students that when they have finished deleting, selecting, and combining the salient information to include in their summaries, their summaries should be only 10 to 25 percent of the original material's length (1 percent or less for a lengthy novel, of course). If the summary is more than 25 percent of the original text's length, they have not encapsulated enough. If many students are having difficulty paring down the information, it may be a sign that summarizing is not the proper way to handle the text. Be open to that possibility. Summarizing is one of thousands of ways to interact with material, not the only way.

Special Section: Teaching Students to Paraphrase

"But the author already said it the best way," your student complains. "How am I supposed to use different words? Isn't that a waste of time when someone else already figured it out?"

Most of us have heard those sentiments from our students. I want to present paraphrasing in a "special section" because it's a skill that is fundamental to creating summaries, and yet, it's one that's particularly difficult to teach. One reason that students struggle with paraphrasing is because they lack the extended exposure to synonyms and language usage that adults had have. As adults, it's easier for us to paraphrase someone else's words because we have a larger vocabulary and more experience with different kinds of sentence structures. We can be sensitive, then, to students who look like a deer caught in the headlights of an oncoming car when we ask them to paraphrase without plagiarizing. Let's look at some of the ways to help students meet the challenges that paraphrasing presents.

Vocabulary Development

One of the best paraphrasing strategies we can offer students is to help them increase the size and use of their vocabulary. Make vocabulary terms and their synonyms a part of everyday language practice in your classroom. Use the new vocabulary words—large and small—in everyday discussions. Immerse students in the terms; make such use seem natural.

I believe that all teachers—yes, even high school teachers—should post a word bank in their classroom. Word banks are large sheets of mural paper on which we list vocabulary terms from many experiences: words from current events or units of study, interesting words, synonyms and antonyms, and words that stand out for any other reason. When new words are in front of students every day, they use those words. Words that are out of sight are often out of mind. I didn't believe a word bank worked until I tried it one year on my classroom wall. I was astonished by the number of words from the growing word bank that students used in their writings, even when I didn't ask them to.

We internalize vocabulary that we hear and say repeatedly. Something that is internalized tends to be readily accessible—in the "front" of our minds. We don't have to use a reference book. When we mentally store such words and concepts, we increase our flexible thinking about concepts on a page. We easily find substitutions and ways to generalize specific facts; we play with language to fit our needs. It's worth reading a few successful books about vocabulary acquisition and following their suggestions. Janet Allen's *Words, Words, Words* (1999) is very good for teachers of grades 4 through 12.

One particular set of vocabulary words is crucial for writing summaries: transition words. Some students can't write summaries because they can't string together words and thoughts coherently. All they need to be successful are the right transition words—a way to get from one idea to the next. Here is a sample set of words to stress: *such as, again, also, as, as a result, as well as, because, before, between, but, during, even though, finally, first, for example, for this reason, however, if, immediately, in the same way, next, on the one hand, on the other hand, then, therefore, throughout, while,* and *yet.*

Synonym Substitution and Condensing

Most people take one of two basic approaches when paraphrasing: (1) substituting synonyms for existing words or (2) rearranging sentences or combining thoughts that were originally presented in multiple sentences. Give your students ample time to practice these two approaches. To build their fluency with paraphrasing, have them list synonyms for existing words and use both new vocabulary and common words. Also give them two sentences that must be combined into a shorter, general statement. Here's an example:

> ORIGINAL TEXT: Adult giant squid can grow to 60 feet long. They have eyes the size of hubcaps, and some of their neurons are so large they can be seen with the naked eye.

> PARAPHRASED TEXT: Because giant squid can be as long as a bus, every part of them is unusually huge.

These quick synonym generators and sentence encapsulations aren't something students should do a few times in September, then never do again until April. The human brain prunes unused skills, especially during the middle and high school years. If we want students to stay "hardwired," they must practice these techniques throughout the year, keeping the necessary neural networks accessible and well connected.

Providing Models

Another strategy to help students with paraphrasing is to give them several examples of successful paraphrasing and let them copy the structure into their own work.

I can hear some teachers say, "If students copy the model exactly, they'll never learn to think for themselves. They'll never be able to handle all situations that way, only the situations that are similar to the model." This belief is a common fallacy about writing and summarizing. The truth is that we eventually outgrow our models, whether they are models of writing, art, performance, or paraphrasing. Give your students plentiful models of original text with paraphrasing, and allow them to practice those structures on new text. The appendix has examples of text and paraphrasing.

The Headline Technique

Yet another strategy for teaching paraphrasing is to have students take any concept, event, or person and turn the example into a newspaper headline. Although they're often used only to hook readers' interest, headlines must capture the essence of the story in one line. To illustrate, an original text presenting a detailed explanation of photosynthesis might yield the headline, "Light and Chlorophyll Combine to Make Sugar and Oxygen." A detailed explanation of how to divide fractions might become "In Dividing, Second Fraction Does a Flip for Multiplying!"

Extended practice in creating news headlines will help students develop a paraphrasing mindset. Although the actual headline may be a helpful mnemonic for long-term retention, the creation of a line to accurately and completely portray the concepts, events, or people is what results in solid learning. Students critiquing each other's headlines in light of their learning will also help them retain information. By the way, it would be helpful to invite a newspaper editor to visit your class and talk about how headlines are created and how reporters get to the gist of stories.

Active Listening

One more way to open the world of paraphrasing for your students is to use active-listening lessons that are part of conflict resolution training. When we listen to people with whom we have conflicts, we must understand their points before forming our response. One of the most effective starting lines is for the listener to respond "So what you're saying is . . ."

This technique forces us to encapsulate the message with the clear intent of getting it right. Here are some other good openers:

- "So what I'm hearing is . . . "
- "The bottom line, then, seems to be . . . "
- "Let me make sure I have this right. You're saying that . . . "

When it's time to teach paraphrasing in a research unit, ask your students to first role-play the mediation of minor conflicts or use a starter line to summarize or paraphrase what the other person said. After practice sessions, apply similar starting lines to sample text passages:

- "So what the author is saying is . . . "
- "In other words . . . "
- "The gist of it is . . . "

When students practice aloud, as they do with role-playing, they create a mind-set for a useful written summarization.

For an effective pedagogical strategy, show students how easy it is to paraphrase something incorrectly, and why making such errors is frustrating for everyone involved. Repeated evaluation of paraphrasing—done well or done poorly—will help students critique their own work while it's in progress, not just after it's done. Show examples of paraphrasings that distort the text's original meaning and that lead to misinformation, poor learning, wasted time, and damage to the paraphraser's reputation. The Appendix includes sample paraphrasings with various degrees of accuracy or distortion (see page 215). Asking your students to analyze these kinds of samples can help them see the importance of paraphrasing accurately. It can also motivate them to confirm their interpretations with others, which is a valuable practice for all of us.

Conclusion

Sometimes I think Nike® has it right. We find success when we find the courage to "Just Do It." Summarization is a scholarly skill, but it's not a skill for scholars alone. All of us can do it if we're taught the varied forms and given repeated practice and feedback. Sometimes our students struggle a bit, but with each new attempt, they get a little closer to attaining the gift of summarization proficiency. That knowledge primes the student's brain, monitors comprehension, and helps each student process and retain information for longer than next week's quiz, especially if we do it repeatedly throughout the year so that students keep those neural pathways open.

As teachers, we can find ways to make it worth students' while to take positive risks with summarizing. Learning summarizing techniques may be daunting at first, but the payoff is great. As Igor Stravinsky said, "I have learned throughout my life as a composer chiefly through my mistakes and pursuits of false assumptions, not my exposure to founts of wisdom and knowledge." Serving as both a mirror and a sieve, summarization enables students to freely explore ideas and analyze them. It can improve student learning and increase student success in all grade levels and all disciplines. And, as we're about to explore, it can even be a lot of fun.

Part 3

Summarization
Techniques

IF YOU'RE THINKING ABOUT USING SUMMARIZATION AS A REGULAR PART OF YOUR CLASSROOM INSTRUCTION, YOU'VE COME TO THE RIGHT PLACE. This section is a collection of summarization techniques suitable for all disciplines. Almost all fit into more than one category of use (e.g., individual, written, artistic, kinesthetic) and, with a little imagination, all can be adapted and enhanced by you as the teacher or by your students.

The Chart of Summarization Techniques, beginning on the following page, provides an initial reference for the 50 techniques that are listed alphabetically and described in full and with variations in the pages that follow. The category icons identified in the chart also appear on the first page of each technique description so that you can flip through all 50 and quickly find, say, a summarization technique that incorporates artistic expression or an interactive oral summarization technique that also involves physical activity. You can use the techniques verbatim, selectively mix and match them, or adjust them to construct a scaffold for each student's unique needs. Many of the techniques already offer initial mixing and scaffolding to get you started.

When you use summarization techniques—at the beginning, middle, or end of a unit or lesson—is, of course, up to you. And it doesn't matter if your students' learning experience involves reading text, watching a video, touring on a field trip, participating in a simulation activity, creating masterful artwork, or memorizing by rote. These techniques will prove their worth as useful tools within any discipline because, through summarization, you will be able to improve each student's comprehension and give each student's long-term memory the boost it needs.

This is only an introductory list of possible summarization techniques. Start and maintain a collection of techniques that work for you or that you'd like to use some day, and put the list within easy reach of your lesson plan book. Many of the techniques I suggest can serve as warm-up or "early bird" activities at the beginning of class, as anchor activities within a differentiated classroom, or as "sponge" activities to soak up dead or transitional time and replace it with substantive interactions related to the day's lesson.

▶ Chart of Summarization Techniques

Technique	Individual	Oral/Interactive	Written	Artistic/Performance	Kinesthetic	Short	Extended
3-2-1	X		X			X	
Acronyms	X		X			X	
Advance Organizers	X		X			X	
Analysis Matrices and Graphic Organizers	X		X	X		X	X
Backwards Summaries	X		X			X	
Bloom's Taxonomy Summary Cubes	X		X	X		X	X
Body Analogies		X		X	X	X	
Body Sculpture		X		X	X	X	
Build a Model	X			X	X		X

► Chart of Summarization Techniques

(continued)

Technique	Individual	Oral/ Interactive	Written	Artistic/ Performance	Kinesthetic	Short	Extended
Camp Songs		X		X	X		X
Carousel Brainstorming		X	X		X	X	X
Charades		X		X	X	X	
Concrete Spellings	X			X		X	
Design a Test	X		X				X
Exclusion Brainstorming	X		X			X	
The Frayer Model	X		X				
Human Bingo		X			X		X
Human Continuum		X			X		X

▶ Chart of Summarization Techniques

(continued)

Technique	Individual	Oral/Interactive	Written	Artistic/Performance	Kinesthetic	Short	Extended
Inner or Outer Circle		X			X		X
Jigsaws		X			X		X
Learning Logs and Journals	X		X	X			X
Lineup		X			X	X	
Luck of the Draw	X	X	X			X	
Moving Summarizations		X	X		X	X	X
Multiple Intelligences	X	X	X	X	X	X	X
One-Word Summaries	X		X			X	
P-M-I		X	X			X	X

▶ Chart of Summarization Techniques

(continued)

Technique	Individual	Oral/ Interactive	Written	Artistic/ Performance	Kinesthetic	Short	Extended
Partners A and B		X			X	X	
Point of View	X		X				X
P-Q-R-S-T	X		X				X
RAFT	X		X				X
Save the Last Word for Me		X					X
Share One; Get One		X	X		X	X	
Socratic Seminars		X	X		X		X
Something-Happened– and-Then/Somebody- Wanted-But-So	X		X			X	
Sorting Cards	X				X	X	

► Chart of Summarization Techniques

(continued)

Technique	Individual	Oral/ Interactive	Written	Artistic/ Performance	Kinesthetic	Short	Extended
Spelling Bee de Strange		X					X
SQ3R	X		X				X
Summarization Pyramids	X	X	X			X	
Summary Ball					X	X	
Synectic Summaries	X		X			X	X
T-Chart/T-List	X		X			X	
Taboo®	X	X	X				X
Test Notes	X		X				X
Think-Pair-Share		X				X	

► Chart of Summarization Techniques

(continued)

Technique	Individual	Oral/ Interactive	Written	Artistic/ Performance	Kinesthetic	Short	Extended
Traditional Rules-Based Summaries	X		X				X
Triads	X	X				X	X
Unique Summarization Assignments	X	X	X	X	X	X	X
Verbs? Change Them!	X		X				X
Word Splash		X	X		X		X

3-2-1

This technique is versatile and relatively quick. You can use it for any situation and in oral, artistic, or written forms. It's a very popular format for exit cards in differentiated classrooms.

Basic Sequence

For the written version, ask your students to write the numerals 3, 2, and 1 down the left side of their paper (a half sheet is fine), leaving a few lines of space between each number. Then post or announce prompts for each number, asking students to write three of something, two of something, and then one of something. For example, students might explain three new things they learned from the lesson, two areas in which they are still confused, and one way they might apply what they've learned to another area. The specific prompts will vary with the lesson content and your instructional goals, but many teachers make the "one item" task more challenging than the "three item" task.

Here are examples from three disciplines (history, math, and science):

3 – Identify three characteristics of Renaissance art that are different from those of art in the Middle Ages.

2 – List two important scientific debates that occurred during the Renaissance.

1 – Provide one good reason that "rebirth" is an appropriate term to describe the Renaissance.

3 – List three applications for slope, y-intercept knowledge in the professional world.

2 – Identify two skills that someone must have to determine slope and y-intercept from a set of points on a plane.

1 – If (x^1, y^1) are the coordinates of a point *W* in a plane, and (x^2, y^2) are the coordinates of a different point *Y*, then the slope of line *WY* is what?

3 – Identify at least three differences between acids and bases.
2 – List two uses of acids and two uses of bases.
1 – State one reason knowledge of acids and bases is important to citizens in our community.

Variations and Extended Applications

The 3, 2, and 1 of something can also be expressed artistically or orally. For those versions, follow the same sequence but change the medium with which students express themselves. Also consider allowing students to choose their mode of expression.

Acronyms

Poor old Aunt Sally. She's constantly making mistakes in the mathematical order of operations. You'll have to excuse her, especially if you already understand when to focus on each operation: parentheses, exponents, multiplication, division, addition, subtraction.

"Please Excuse My Dear Aunt Sally" is an extension of PEMDAS, the classic acronym for the order of mathematical operations. Its mnemonic fortitude has helped numerous students over the years. PEMDAS is clearly a memory aid because it's a distillation from a lesson on order of operations. When you think about it, though, PEMDAS is also a summarization. Creating acronyms for concepts, cycles, protocols, sequences, and systems is a great way to summarize.

Basic Sequence

Begin by asking students to list the essential attributes of something you are teaching them. For example, say you've been focusing on how to write great introductions to essays. In response to your prompt, your students might create this list:

- Hook the reader with something compelling.
- Establish common ground with the reader.
- Provide background information to set the stage for your focused thesis.
- Narrow the topic to a thesis statement.
- Reflect the organization of the thinking that follows.

Next, ask students to look at each listed attribute and identify a single term to use as a key word for remembering that attribute. I like doing this as a group activity because discussing and deciding on key words provides another opportunity for summarization. Key words for remembering how to write good essay introductions might be *hook, common, information, thesis,* and *reflect.*

Now it's a matter of sequencing the letters in an order that makes sense. If the attributes are things that don't need to be in a specific sequence, such as Egyptian inventions, types of trees, or characteristics of particular operating systems, then it's a relatively easy process of moving the letters around until something coherent and meaningful emerges. If the sequence is set, such as the steps in a math problem, the process of how a bill goes through Congress, or the metamorphosis of mealworms, the order of the letters is nonnegotiable and creating a memorable acronym can be a bit more challenging, although I find that students usually manage amazingly well.

So how would students create an acronym to summarize writing an introduction to an essay? The starting letters for the key attributes we've identified are *h*(ook), *c*(ommon), *i*(nformation), *t*(hesis), and *r*(eflect). Sequence is not a factor because great introductions feature all these components in any order. Therefore, a number of acronyms come to mind: RICHT, THRIC, CHRIT, CIRTH, TRICH, and CHIRT. For example, "CIRTH" could stand for "Careful Introductions Really Thrill." "TRICH" could stand for "Tri Compelling Hooks." "RICHT" could stand for "Real Insights Can Hold Together." You or your students might come up with something even more meaningful.

If students are struggling with the task, ask them to consider a different key word. In the essay introduction example, I could have used *cg* for "common ground" instead of just *c*. This slight modification might expose new acronyms for students' summarizations.

Variations and Extended Applications

This technique also works as a prelearning activity. You might create an initial list of attributes as a whole-class activity, then have students revise the lists on their own (another opportunity for summarizing). As mnemonic devices, acronyms can be even more powerful when created by the students themselves. If appropriate, ask each student to design his or her own acronyms for something to be studied, then vote on the top three and photocopy them for everyone. The voting criteria should include clarity, accuracy, and completeness, plus whether or not the acronym is memorable.

Advance Organizers

Instructional scaffolding is a way of providing students with templates, direct instruction, and other tools that can help them to succeed. It's comparable to holding a student's hand while she walks along a balance beam in physical education, or acting as a copresenter when he gives his first oral report in history class. Eventually, though, the idea is to wean students off such direct support and let them "fly solo."

Providing students with a fill-in-the-blank-style advance organizer (see Figure 1) is a great scaffolding move that also serves as a summarization device.

— Figure 1 —
Advance Organizer: Dividing Mixed Numbers

Working independently, fill in the blanks below.

When dividing mixed numbers, we must first turn each mixed number into a _____ _____. Once done, we change the operation from division to _____. Now, we multiply the first fraction by the _____ of the second fraction. If our final answer is a top-heavy or an _____ fraction, then we rewrite it as a _____ _____, and we reduce it to _____ terms.

Basic Sequence

In advance, write your own summarization of the material you're presenting. Then review what you've written and make a second draft, replacing key words and phrases with blank lines.

Either during or after the learning process, ask students to complete these fill-in-the-blank organizers by writing in the correct terms. If appropriate and if time allows, they might share their responses with a classmate and agree on the best answers.

Every time I use this technique with my students, I have a specific idea of what word or phrase goes in each blank, and every time one or more students will show me how the blank could be interpreted differently and how something else can fit logically into the space. Be open to that possibility. Students have a lot to teach us.

Variations and Extended Applications

For students who are ready for something more complex, be strategic in what you remove. Provide blank spaces that you know could be filled in with more than one possibility or that will require students to use a bit more logic and a few more context clues before they decide on the best response.

A related summarization technique is to have students create advance organizers for each other. After they have filled in the blanks to create a summary, a good next step is to ask them to express their summaries artistically. They might create an acronym with the inserted words or design a crossword puzzle, which will require them to think of clues in addition to the schematic puzzles. (Please don't allow students to use computerized puzzle generators.) Completing crossword puzzles created by a classmate can also be worthwhile, although it doesn't incorporate summarization as much as generating them does.

Analysis Matrices and Graphic Organizers

A person's ability to retrieve information accurately and completely has a lot to do with how it first enters her mind when she is learning it. As teachers, we owe it to our students and communities to use our subject expertise to present curriculum in a coherent manner that will be meaningful to students. An added aspect in all of this structuring is that society as a whole is predominantly visual in its orientation (Hyerle, 2000). For this reason, I'm an advocate of presenting concepts, facts, and skills in visual formats at least once during every unit of study.

Many of us already structure material for our students. Various examples include when we write the causes of an event on the chalkboard and draw arrows pointing to their effects; when we place a box around important concepts we've posted; when we provide a template for creating an essay's outline or solving an algebra problem; and when we post a time line of events, a pie graph, or a mind map in which we follow a subject's development or a person's thinking. We even give students graph paper when they are first learning to line up columns in mathematics. What makes analysis matrices and graphic organizers so great for summarization is that their formats are so adaptable: useful in all stages of learning and for a variety of purposes.

Basic Sequence

As you begin a unit or lesson, provide students with a matrix or another graphic way to organize the information they are about to encounter. Students' attempts to complete the structure as a prelearning activity can prime their brains and create anticipation. For example, Figure 2 shows an anticipation guide that will help to structure students' initial thinking about Erich Remarque's *All Quiet on the Western Front* before they turn to page 1.

— FIGURE 2 — Analysis Matrix: Themes in *All Quiet on the Western Front*			
Themes in the Book	**My Opinion**	**My Group's Opinion**	**The Author's Opinion**
Nature is indifferent to mankind's pain and decisions.			
"To no man does the earth mean so much as to the soldier."			
Cruel trainers make the most useful trainers for soldiers about to go to war.			
War forces people to reject traditional values and civilized behavior.			
"This book is to be neither an accusation nor a confession, and least of all an adventure."			
"Every soldier believes in Chance."			
Friendships endure all.			

Likewise, the row headings in Figure 3 show students what to look for as they read an article on the components of blood—and the cell contents show how one student might complete it after having read the assigned material.

Analysis matrices are also great for helping students to develop patterns of understanding. Figure 4 shows a completed matrix for studying pronouns and a filled-in organizer designed to help students apply the understanding that subjective pronouns always perform the action of the verb and objective pronouns always receive the action of the verb.

A data retrieval-style analysis matrix, like the one in Figure 5 (see page 50), provides an easy way for students to take notes and monitor their progress during a unit of study. It also enables students, with the teacher's help, to narrow the focus of their research and to quickly identify where they need more information. They can walk into the library or go to the Internet with the skeleton or outline already created.

— FIGURE 3 —
Analysis Matrix: Attributes of Blood

Questions to Ask	Red Cells	White Cells	Plasma	Platelets
Purpose?	Carry O2, nutrients	Fight disease	Substrate	Clot blood
Amount?	5 million per cubic millimeter	A few thousand per cubic millimeter	9 pints in an adult man, 7 pints in an adult woman	Short-lived, ?
Size and Shape?	Round little donuts, indented center	Large, blobby	Yellowish fluid, made of water, salt, protein	Fibrin, fibrinogen (fiber-like)
Nucleus?	No, not in mature state	Yes	No	?
Where Formed?	Bone marrow, spleen	Spleen, liver, lymph nodes	Osmotic forces at capillary wall, water enters blood	Bone marrow

— FIGURE 4 —
Analysis Matrix and Application: Personal Pronouns

Personal Pronouns		Subjective	Objective	Possessive	Reflexive
Singular	1st	I	me	my mine	myself
	2nd	you	you	your(s)	yourself
	3rd	he she it	him her it	his hers its	himself herself itself
Plural	1st	we	us	our(s)	ourselves
	2nd	you	you	your(s)	yourselves
	3rd	they	them	their(s)	themselves

1st person, singular: __I__ hit the ball. The ball hit __me__. The ball is __mine__. __I__ looked in the mirror ball and saw __myself__.

2nd person, singular: __You__ hit the ball. The ball hit __You__. The ball is __yours__. __You__ looked in the mirror ball and saw __yourself__.

3rd person, singular (masculine): __He__ hit the ball. The ball hit __him__. __He__ looked in the mirror ball and saw __himself__.

— FIGURE 5 —
Analysis Matrix: Data Retrieval Chart

Topic of Study: _____

Information Sources	Question #1	Question #2	Question #3	Question #4
Source 1				
Source 2				
Source 3				
Source 4				

Variations and Extended Applications

A teacher's best move may be to present a variety of analysis matrices and graphic organizers and then allow students to choose the most appropriate one for the summarizing or processing at hand. For example, if their task is to compare and contrast two concepts, there are many ways to do it graphically. Figure 6 and Figure 7 show two graphic organizers formats that have worked for my students.

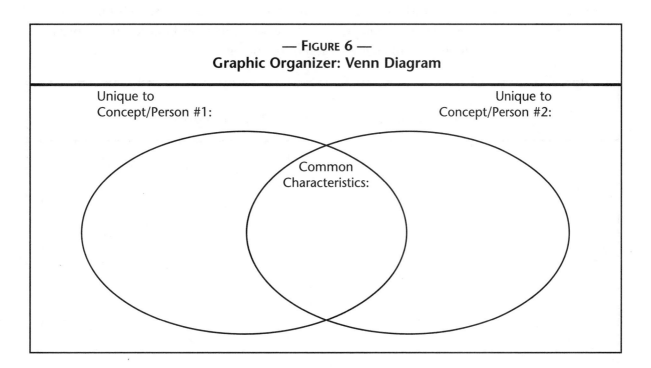

— FIGURE 6 —
Graphic Organizer: Venn Diagram

Unique to
Concept/Person #1:

Unique to
Concept/Person #2:

Common
Characteristics:

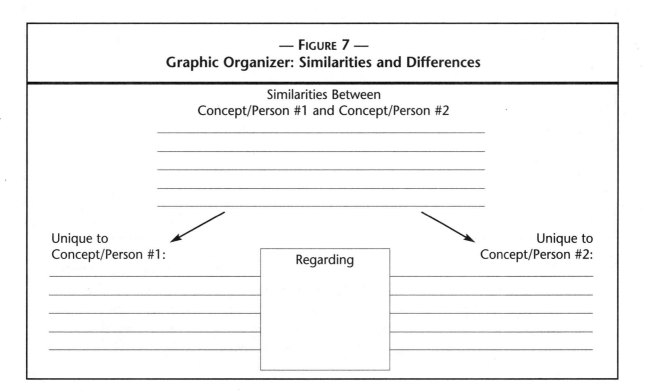

— FIGURE 7 —
Graphic Organizer: Similarities and Differences

Similarities Between
Concept/Person #1 and Concept/Person #2

Unique to
Concept/Person #1:

Unique to
Concept/Person #2:

Regarding

When students need to analyze the attributes of something or someone, such as a character in a novel or an historical figure, an organizer like the one in Figure 8 can be very helpful.

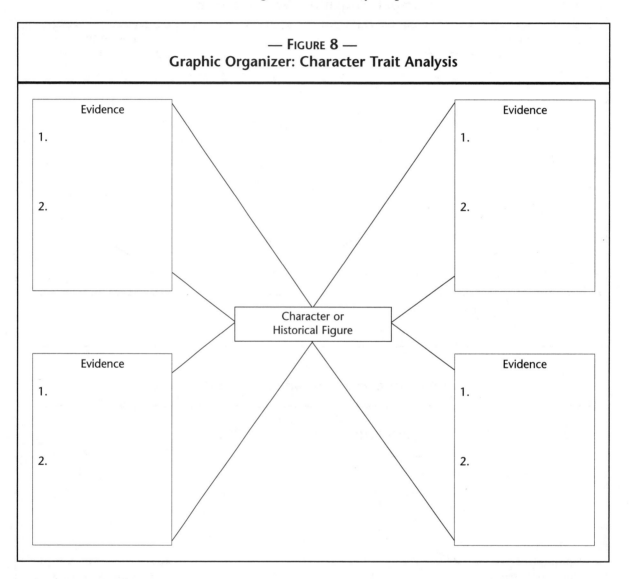

— FIGURE 8 —
Graphic Organizer: Character Trait Analysis

As shown in Figure 9, ideas that require exploration in a number of directions might be expressed using a cluster or web or a similar form known as the "wheel and spokes," or "mind-mapping," which has long been used for outlining. And don't forget organizers for cycles or sequences, such as the flow chart in Figure 10 (see page 54).

— **FIGURE 9**—
Graphic Organizer: Cluster Graphics

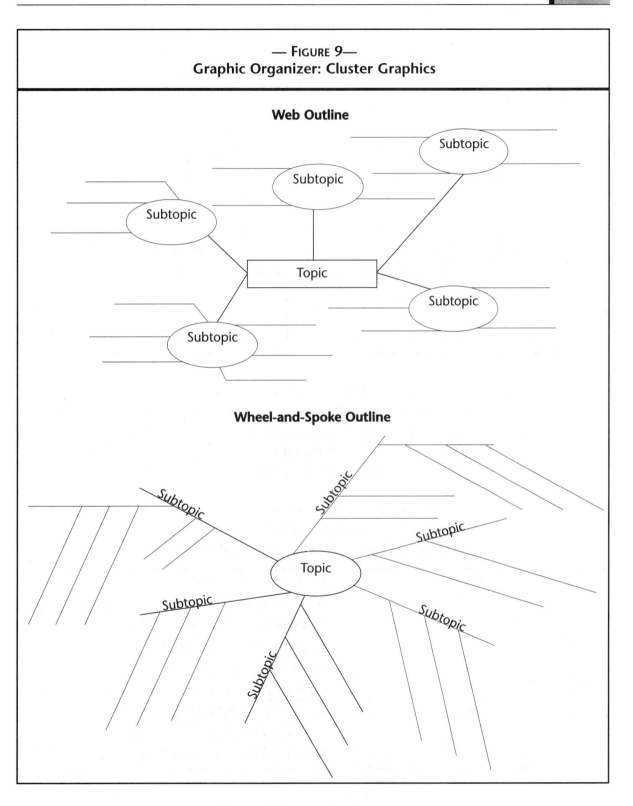

Web Outline

Wheel-and-Spoke Outline

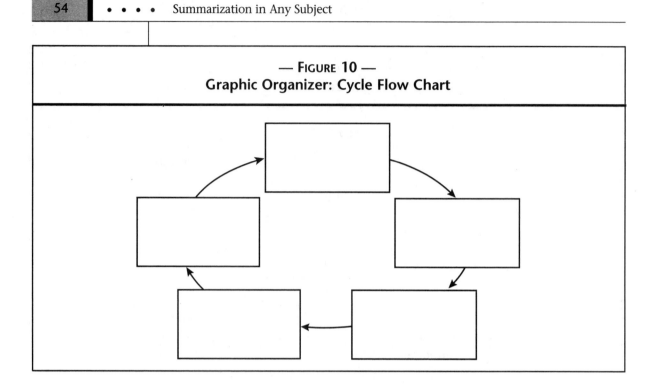

— FIGURE 10 —
Graphic Organizer: Cycle Flow Chart

Expository writings, such as essays, often benefit from some kind of schematic planning. The structure in Figure 11 is a good choice. And for cause-and-effect or action-and-results, students might use something that looks like Figure 12. Or they might reverse the words by placing the cause in the center and surrounding it with multiple effects.

— FIGURE 11 —
Graphic Organizer: Topics and Subtopics

Main Idea (Topic Sentence)	Subtopic #1	Supporting Detail/Evidence for Subtopic #1
		Supporting Detail/Evidence for Subtopic #1
		Supporting Detail/Evidence for Subtopic #1
	Subtopic #2	Supporting Detail/Evidence for Subtopic #2
		Supporting Detail/Evidence for Subtopic #2
		Supporting Detail/Evidence for Subtopic #2
	Subtopic #3	Supporting Detail/Evidence for Subtopic #3
		Supporting Detail/Evidence for Subtopic #3
		Supporting Detail/Evidence for Subtopic #3

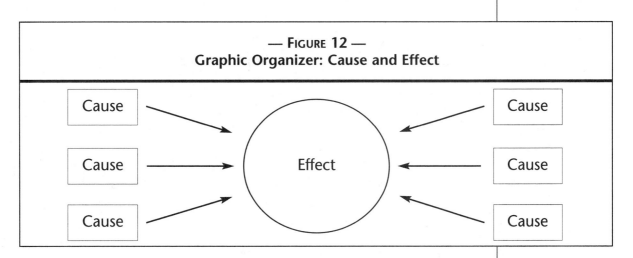

— FIGURE 12 —
Graphic Organizer: Cause and Effect

Finally, if students need help structuring their thoughts to decide on a particular topic of study, the organizer in Figure 13 (see page 56) provides great support.

Sometimes students will invent their own hybrid formats or come up with a brand new graphic organizer. Let them use their creations and decide later whether or not it was successful. Deviating from a teacher's suggestions after serious contemplation is usually progress, not defiance.

These are just a few of the many possibilities for matrices and graphic organizers. There are a number of great resources for teachers interested in using such techniques to help prime, process, and summarize information with students. I particularly recommend Allen (1999); Forsten, Grant, and Hollas (2003); Frender (1990); Hyerle (2000, 2004); Black and Parks (1990); Stephens and Brown (2000); Strong, Silver, Perini, and Tuculescu (2002); Vacca and Vacca (2005); and Wood and Harmon (2001).

In our busy teacher worlds, it's easy to forget the power of structuring information in a graphic way. We do it readily for younger children, but too often think that middle and high school students can create such structures for themselves; they often can't. As experts in our subject areas, we have the perspective and savvy to bring it all together in formats that increase understanding and long-term retention. Our goal isn't just to present knowledge to students; it's to present knowledge so that students can understand it and find meaning in it. Analysis matrices and graphic organizers help us to transform our role from mere presenters to true teachers.

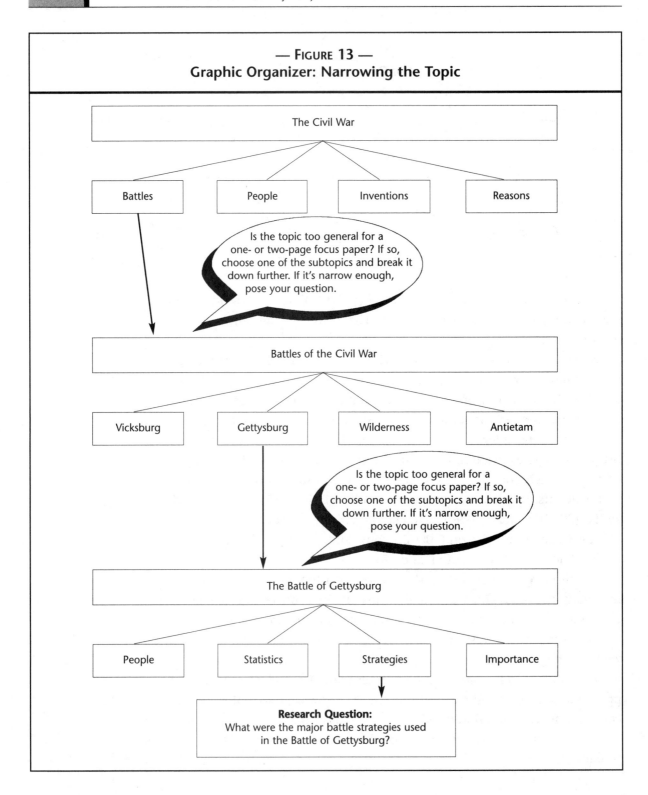

— FIGURE 13 —
Graphic Organizer: Narrowing the Topic

Backwards Summaries

Lots of teachers with good intentions begin their units by focusing on the smaller elements of their topic. From there, they skillfully show how those elements come together to create slightly larger components of the topic, then how those components form the larger pieces of the topic's main body of knowledge, and finally, how all the larger pieces create a full picture of what they're teaching. At that point, they turn it over to the students and say, "Now create a complete model of this topic yourself." Many students respond with a blank stare; they don't get it.

To illustrate, many of us who have taught essay-writing have done so by first focusing on words, phrases, and grammar, then graduating to sentences. Next, we've asked students to put the sentences together to create paragraphs, then to put the paragraphs together according to a theme to create a polished essay. Step one led to step two, and step two led to step three.

Unfortunately, this approach can prevent students from having their own "Aha!" moments. Wise teachers maximize learning by simultaneously reversing the expected order—asking students to explore ideas both from the basic level to the most complex level *and* from the most complex level back to the basics. This is one of the tenets of constructivism. The idea of backwards summaries is to have students start with the final product, the "big picture" view, and then go on to explore the smaller components and their meanings, while also studying those components and working toward the big picture.

Basic Sequence

Offer your students summarization experiences in which you give them the final version of something explained, performed, or presented well.

Then have them comment on the criteria for overall success, the effects of specific components on the product's quality or personal achievement, or the early steps in the product's development or personal achievement. The following prompts will give you a good idea about how to kick off the process:

- "Make the web from which this paragraph came."

- "Here's the completed math solution. What would happen if I had never considered the absolute value of x?"

- "Here's the final French translation of this sentence. What if I had not checked the tense of each verb?"

- "Here's a well-constructed concerto. What happens if I remove the oboe's eight measures on page 4?"

- "Here's a well-done lab procedure. What happens if I don't use distilled water?"

When students bring together discrete pieces to create a new whole, such analysis will illuminate more about how to create something than will synthesis experiences alone. Students need analysis and synthesis, induction and deduction, and learning forwards and backwards.

Variations and Extended Applications

Students respond well to both inductive and deductive approaches, even if presented at the same time. Inductive lessons usually move from the specific to the general, while deductive lessons begin with the general and move to the specific. One of the big differences between the two is the differing foundations for their claims: inductive reasoning relies on observations and experiences while deductive reasoning relies on rules, laws, principles, and accepted theories. Here are two examples to clarify the two types of thinking:

- *Inductive reasoning:* If you notice that it hurts every time a bee stings you, you can assume it will hurt in the future when a bee stings you.

- *Deductive reasoning:* If you are aware that when a bee stings you, it injects a small irritant (poison) into you that causes pain, you can conclude it will hurt you when a bee stings you in the future.

In backwards summaries, we can provide both experiences: experiential foundations upon which to draw conclusions, as well as the established big picture concepts, principles, and rules from with which we can reasonably predict what will happen or make inferences. Students need both inductive and deductive experiences to fully grasp many concepts they are taught.

Bloom's Taxonomy Summary Cubes

Teachers can use Bloom's taxonomy of higher order thinking in many ways to help students summarize and interact with what they've learned. One way is Bloom's taxonomy summary cubes, which provide creative, hands-on activities and promote substantive review and reflection. The cubes also meet the needs of those students who respond best to kinesthetic experiences. And they look good displayed in the classroom, too.

Basic Sequence

Distribute poster board, rulers, glue or tape, and scissors, and ask your students to make cubes with each side at least five inches long. Have them record each level of Bloom's taxonomy on each of the six faces: *Recall* (knowledge), *Comprehension, Application, Analysis, Synthesis,* and *Evaluation.* They'll need to make the titles fairly small so they will have room to make notations (or draw pictures) on each face—interpretations of the topic, based on the particular taxonomy level.

While students are constructing their cubes, distribute or post a list of suggested ways to manifest each level of Bloom's taxonomy. Such explanations or definitions are fairly common and readily available on the Internet. To refresh your memory, Figure 14 shows a basic definition of each level, followed by example assignments or prompts.

Provide students with a list of sample prompts keyed to the content and ask them to choose a way to express what they've learned about a topic for each level.

— FIGURE 14 —
Bloom's Taxonomy Levels and Sample Prompts

Level	Explanation	Sample Prompts
Recall	Students cite content they remember.	• What color was the dress? • How old was the president at the time? • What is the formula for . . . ? • What were the author's two arguments? • In what year did . . . ? • What are the four steps in the process?
Comprehension	Students demonstrate whether or not they understand a topic.	• What is a clear example of each category . . . ? • Which actions support the government's policy in . . . ? • Can you explain how . . . ? • Can you classify the items according to . . . ? • Which word doesn't fit? • Why did . . . ? • Can you translate an English poem into Spanish? • What's the difference between X and Y?
Application	Students use knowledge and skills in different situations.	• Predict what would happen if we changed . . . • Use the formulas to determine . . . • Create a proposal for . . . • Explain how a literary device changed the tone of the novel. • Offer solutions to a problem.
Analysis	Students break down topics into component pieces and analyze them in the context of the whole.	• Can you defend the character's decision to . . . ? • What is the function of . . . ? • How did the theorist arrive at his theory? • Can you rank the arguments in order of importance? • Which comment seems the most sincere? • Which variables had the biggest effect? • Can you identify the mistake in . . . ? • What's the relationship between X and Y?

— FIGURE 14 —
Bloom's Taxonomy Levels and Sample Prompts   *(continued)*

Level	Explanation	Sample Prompts
Synthesis	Students bring together seemingly contradictory aspects or topics to form something new.	• Add a character to the scene and explain how it would change the outcome. • Write a song that teaches students about . . . • Create and present a public service announcement that convinces viewers to . . . • Create a cartoon that depicts . . . • Design a better system or process for . . .
Evaluation	Students use all the other levels to judge the validity, success, or value of something, given specific criteria.	• Can you judge the value of . . . ? • Which essay succeeds and why? • Did the group meet its goal? Explain why or why not. • Which process is most efficient and why? • Is this lobbying group in compliance with the law? Explain your judgment. • Could this policy have worked 20 years ago? If so, why; if not, why not? • Which decision is unethical?

Here is an example of how one student might create a summary cube based on the U.S. Bill of Rights:

Face 1: *Recall*
Student records one of the first six Amendments from the Bill of Rights.

Face 2: *Comprehension*
Student writes an explanation of why the Amendment he chose for Face 1 was so important to the authors of the Bill of Rights.

Face 3: *Application*
Student draws a picture or creates a small collage of magazine pictures that depicts the Amendment being applied to everyday life.

Face 4: *Analysis*

Student identifies a modern-day situation in which strict adherence to the Amendment would prove hurtful.

Face 5: *Synthesis*

Student explains how another culture might feel toward such a right, and how legislators in that culture might change the Amendment's wording to better meet their culture's preferences and values.

Face 6: *Evaluation*

Student indicates whether he believes this Amendment still serves us well today, and he is prepared to explain his thinking to the rest of the class.

Variations and Extended Applications

Depending on your schedule and students' readiness levels, you may want to provide more or less specific prompts (or a smaller selection of possible prompts) for each face. You could also challenge students to come up with their own prompts, based on their understanding of the various taxonomy levels. Remember to consider various ways of expression: written, artistic, and oral. Try to set aside time for students to share their cubes with their classmates.

In some education circles, Bloom's taxonomy has become a cliché because it is overly referenced in daily teaching. Some people find it stale. That's too bad, because Bloom's taxonomy certainly is a great example of something worth revisiting over and over again, if for no reason other than as a wake-up call to raise the complexity of our questioning and assignments. On a very practical level, using the taxonomy in a cube summarization is good practice because students learn the material.

Body Analogies

Most students are body-centric—very focused on their own bodies—and it makes sense to use this interest to aid learning. If we can connect learning to their bodies, students may tune in a bit more and may remember material for a longer time. In Part 2, we discussed one example of a body analogy summarization: my students' comparison of Boss Tweed with the human heart. Figure 15 provides a general guide to body analogies. The examples listed are just a sampling of what you and your students might come up with.

Summarization occurs in more than one place with this technique: first, when students are making analogies, and again, when they are presenting their analogies to others—defending their ideas against critics. It's a highly effective way for them to interact with what they're learning.

Basic Sequence

Ask students to form groups and to identify a way or ways in which the lesson's subject is analogous to parts of the human body (again, minus the genitalia). At first, groups will need some guidance, so be prepared to give it. Invite them to list first the critical attributes of the concept they're trying to connect to the body, then to look for body parts that might best represent that concept. Some groups may find it easier to reverse that direction: to first identify unique characteristics of specific body parts, then to see how those characteristics fit with the concepts being learned. Either way, the discussion will be a good review of material.

The next step is expressing the analogies. You might hold a large-group discussion with the students pointing to their own bodies or classmates' bodies as they explain the analogies they've generated. You could also ask students to draw a human body on an 8^1/$_2$" × 11" sheet of paper

Body Part	Possible Analogies	Examples
Finger or Hands	Artwork, dexterity, flexibility, omnidirectional aspects, or work that can be done collectively, as well as individually	Machines composed of individual parts that work to create a single product; sports players on a team; ant colonies; the three branches of the U.S. government; different labor unions collaborating to overcome worker abuse during the Industrial Revolution
Feet	Anything requiring "footwork" or a journey	Gathering supplies or data; setting up a problem or a lab; reflecting on a philosophy or argument before confronting someone else; military scouting in pre-20th century warfare; a minor character whose actions enable a major character to do something; transition words like *however, finally, on the other hand,* and *therefore* that carry the flow of thinking from one sentence to another
Heart	Anything that expresses feeling, forcing, life, passion, pumping, rhythm, or supplying	The basic principles of a government, philosophy, or religion; sodium-potassium ion pump that conducts the impulse down the length of the axon; a major character of a novel around which the story revolves or a major figure in an historical event; right triangle for the Pythagorean Theorem; isolating the variable to solve algebraic equations; the sun in our solar system; the thermal vents in the mid-Atlantic Ridge
Spine or Skeleton	Anything that provides structure, support, or both	The motif of a story on which the author has placed the "flesh" of plot and characterization; a data retrieval chart for taking notes; cytoplasm in a cell; armature in clay sculpture; an algorithm for math problems; the townspeople and culture for the conflicts in a novel; the interior workings of a company or government; the infrastructure of a country; a Local Area Network (LAN); taxonomy and nomenclature charts

— FIGURE 15 —
A Guide to Body Analogies

— FIGURE 15 —
A Guide to Body Analogies   *(continued)*

Body Part	Possible Analogies	Examples
Rib Cage or Cranium	Anything that protects	The hull of a ship; law enforcement agencies; armed forces; a cell wall or membrane; the bark of a tree; the absolute value of a number; parentheses' role in math equations (order of operations); defining a problem clearly; specific rules for something like determining the areas to shade when graphing inequalities; a country's rules as stated in its constitution
Pancreas or Stomach	Anything that processes or breaks down other things	Antagonists in a novel; "Mother Nature" (flood, earthquake, fire, tornado, age, rust, infection, radiation, gravity, lack of oxygen); computer viruses; decomposers in the energy transfer cycle; breaking down polynomial expressions into their component binomials; chromatography paper; outlining text
Liver	Any kind of filter	A specific point of view; an alternative perspective; public opinion; evaluation rubrics; theories to consider; approving scientific methods; a sieve; analysis of an idea or object; Net Nanny (Internet filtering services)
Esophagus	Anything that pushes things along in wavelike motion	A sequence of events pushing a character or historical personage closer a conflict or a resolution; a time line; the Marshall Plan to rebuild Europe after World War II; "Manifest Destiny" of U.S. westward expansion
Skin	Anything that protects something else or that regenerates and is renewed	Politics (Washington, D.C., when a new presidential administration arrives); the hull of a ship; a driver's license; new versions of software; crab legs; businesses with new advertising and promotional techniques; a public or historical figure's persona; an opinion or theory that is elastic enough to accommodate multiple views without breaking

or to make a large body outline on mural or butcher paper using a class-mate's body as the template. (These larger examples are a lot of fun and look great hanging in the classroom.) Once student groups have drawn their body outlines (stick figures are fine), ask them to write a small para-graph explaining each analogy somewhere on the paper and to draw a line from the paragraph to the analogous body part.

Variations and Extended Applications

Because some analogies may only partially portray a concept being learned, you might ask students to make more than one analogy, each focused on a different body part. And for added complexity, invite stu-dents to consider how variations of body position can communicate distinct meanings. Think of the different messages expressed by bodies displayed with arms and legs reaching out to resemble a starfish, bodies leaning on something else for support, or bodies in a fetal position. Students may have chosen hands to illustrate a certain politically ideol-ogy, for example. Should the hands be drawn as fists, or with open fin-gers? These are questions that invite serious analysis.

Finally, for many students, using the body—drawn or real—is a great mnemonic device for remembering facts. They associate different facts with body parts that are different but are also a portion of a larger, coher-ent system. Thus, students become their own study guides—walking encyclopedias of knowledge. Ask them about cosine/sine/tangent, African caravans, or conjugating irregular –*ir* verbs in Spanish, and they will pat and point to various body parts as they remember all of the information. I've seen this going on during tests, too. It can be very entertaining, although it's *definitely* something you want to warn a substitute about, should you ever be absent on a test day.

Body Sculpture

In the body sculpture technique, also known as the statues technique, groups of students determine the essential attributes of a concept, idea, process, fact, sequence, or skill, and then design a frozen tableau using all the group members' bodies in a way that best represents those essentials. Although they have a lot of fun molding their classmates' bodies into an assembly of "statues" to represent what everyone has learned about a topic, there's more than fun going on here. The analytical discussions students have while creating the sculpture and the discussions that their classmates have about the finished tableaus help the information move into long-term memory.

Let's eavesdrop on a group of students using this technique.

"If you put your arms over your head like a roof, we'll have shelter," Mario suggested.

"Yeah, but what if I want to be something else instead?" Lakiesha replied.

"Fine. What else is there?"

Lakiesha scanned the textbook page a moment before pointing to the paragraph at the bottom right corner. "Look here. It says that the second component of a habitat is food."

"How are you going to show it?" Dylan asked.

"I could just freeze mid-motion while I rub my stomach," Lakiesha replied.

Mario nodded. "OK. Now, how can we show decomposers?" he asked.

"Wait a minute," Terry interjected. "That's not a part of a habitat."

"Yes, it is," Mario said. "You can't have a habitat without decomposers."

"Well, yes, uh, no, I mean, I dunno," Terry stammered. "What I mean is that we're supposed to sculpt the five basic elements of a habitat. Decomposers is on the next page under 'Energy Cycle,' not under 'Elements of a Habitat.' From what I read, I think the elements are food, water, shelter, space, and arrangement of those things. Decomposers are not a basic element of an animal's habitat."

"Yeah," Arnold added. "The book said decomposers enter the picture only after something is dead. Animals don't have a death habitat, only a life habitat."

"OK, I get it," Mario said, nodding. "So Lakiesha represents food, and I'll be the shelter. What do the rest of you want to be?"

"I'll be water," Anna offered, "but first, I want to know something: Are there habitats that don't have decomposers?"

"I don't know," Terry said. "I suppose there could be."

Anna continued. "I was thinking of little creatures in the frozen tundra that stay alive in the frozen soil and break down a dead animal's remains, releasing energy back into the system. How can they do that when it's so cold?"

"And what about animals that die in the middle of the ocean and their remains sink more than a mile to the bottom of the ocean?" Jason added. "What decomposers live in places that have several tons of pressure on every square inch of their bodies?"

"OK, OK," Mario cut in. "We can look at the next chapter of the textbook when we're done. Let's get back to basic habitat elements. Terry, can you read them off again?"

Basic Sequence

After your students have encountered some information—read a textbook chapter, listened to a lecture, watched a movie, done sample problems, watched a demonstration—and after you have discussed the material briefly as a large group, divide the students into small groups of four to six. Then ask them to "sculpt" a representation of one of the topics studied—a particular concept, idea, process, fact, sequence, or skill—using every group member's body. You might have all groups use the same topic, or you may wish to assign a different topic to each group.

Give your students time to discuss what the topic's essential attributes are and how best to represent them using every group member's body in a purposeful manner. I recommend limiting discussions to 5 to 10 minutes at the elementary level and 10 to 15 minutes at the middle and high school levels. This might be one of the quietest movement activities a class can do because we teachers secretly share each group's concept, telling members of each group to talk quietly so they don't reveal the concept or suggested representations to other groups. The need to keep things secret will keep the noise level down.

Finally, have the groups form their frozen tableaus one at a time for the rest of the class so that their classmates can analyze the body sculptures and evaluate their accuracy. As the teacher, you facilitate the discussions with questions like these:

- What concept does this body sculpture represent? (This obviously works best when each group has illustrated a different concept.)

- How does this group's body sculpture express that concept?

- Let's see if the sculpture's portrayal is accurate and comprehensive enough. Where in the text (or learning experience) were these attributes described?

- Is there a way to improve this sculpture so it clarifies or widens our understanding of the concept?

- If we were to ask one member of the sculpture group to become a moving part, what would it be and why? How does that movement further the accurate portrayal of the concept?

Here's an example, using the writing term "transition," which refers to words and phrases that move readers smoothly from one sentence to the next. I asked my 7th grade students to list all synonyms for "transition" and to look for one that suggests a physical symbol of it. They settled on the word "bridge," as in "a writer makes a bridge between one idea and another."

They discussed different attributes that were analogous, playing with the term and its meanings. When they were ready, they formed their bodies into a bridge, with one student suspended by two students holding his legs and two students holding his shoulders (a total of five students). The four students on either side of the suspended student completed the picture by striking various poses that represent thinking: one pointed a finger to her temple, one held his fingers in mid-snap as he solved a puzzle, another held a light bulb above her head for an idea, and another pointed her finger to make a point. The suspended student was the bridge between the ideas on either side. The analogy clearly was that a transition word symbolized a bridge that moved the reader from one sentence to another or one idea to another.

One of my student groups created such a sculpture, and the rest of the class accurately identified it as "transition." But one holdout disagreed, saying that the tableau looked the same from either side, whether you looked at it forwards or backwards. For this reason, he thought it might be illustrating another of our vocabulary terms, "palindrome"—a word or number like "radar," "noon," or "45,154" that reads the same when it's reversed. A second student countered that "palindromes don't have ideas on either side of them, so it has to be transition." The first student saw the logic and retracted his statement. That subtlety and degree of thinking would never have taken place if I had approached this vocabulary instruction is a conventional way—say, assigning definitions and telling the kids to use each word in a sentence.

Variations and Extended Applications

A great follow-up activity to body sculpture summarization is to ask students to write about their understanding of the topic in a learning log and to mention how the body sculpting experience enhanced or changed that understanding. To help them internalize the information, you may ask them to draw each body sculpture (stick figures are fine) and to explain how each represents the concepts. It can also be powerful to take a picture of the body sculptures and to post them with descriptions somewhere in the room for continued reference throughout the unit.

Some teachers may be skeptical of body sculpture's ability to summarize more abstract ideas such as democracy, inference, nuance in poetry, the quadratic formula, or integrals. Our students are smarter than we are, especially when working in groups. They will come up with clever representations that we never imagined. It is rare to find a concept that is not "sculptable." Even when students are given topics that seem subtle or esoteric, such as the difference between simile and metaphor, assonance and consonance, indirect democracy versus a republic, principles of economy, a protagonist's change of heart, compound versus simple interest on a loan, and political ideology, to name a few, they will rise to the challenge and sculpt well. Better yet, they'll learn and retain the information, and we teachers will learn as well.

I'll give one final illustration. I once challenged a student group to sculpt the idea of "metamorphosis," using terms like "growth," "change," and "sequence" to clarify the concept. Here's how the group responded: One student curled into a tight ball on the floor while another sat next to him with a straight back, looking up. Another student put herself next to that seated student, but she was up on her knees and was taller than the sitting student and the balled-up classmate. Then a fourth student stood next to the kneeling student with his knees bent and his body lowered slightly. A fifth student stood tall and straight, and by doing so she was taller than any of the other four students. A person looking at this group would see a steadily increasing height—something moving from a curled up ball to a fully formed human child. It accurately represented "metamorphosis," "growth," "change," or "sequence." This particular activity carried even more meaning and usefulness because the endpoint of tallness was represented by one of the shortest students in the room. For once, the shorter child was a symbol of tallness, something she had not often felt.

Build a Model

Remember model building? When you were a student, you may have built a model of the solar system using styrofoam balls or models of molecules using gumdrops and toothpicks. Or if you grew up in California in the '60s, as I did, you probably modeled California missions using clay or sugar cubes. Few of us remember other assignments as vividly; the model-building process is that intense.

Of course, students must be aware that the goal of building models is to learn the content, not play with sugar cubes, clay, gumdrops, or toothpicks. As teachers, we can guild the process to prompt students' reflections about why they built the models the ways they did and what each component represents from their learning.

"Hey, Mr. Smith," Dexter called from across the room. "Check out the mag-lev train I built."

Mr. Smith finished explaining the criteria for success in the robotics module to three 8th graders, then crossed the room to Dexter. "Hey, Dex," he said. "Tell me about your setup here."

"Well, there are three things in my mag-lev model," Dexter began. "First, I have guidance, which is these high wooden rails that stand along the length of the magnet track. They keep the floating magnet stable."

"Why is that necessary?" Mr. Smith asked.

"The magnets repel each other. The floating magnet rides on a kind of bubble above the track magnets. Because the repelling nature is omnidirectional, the floating magnet would be pushed to the sides if I didn't have the retaining walls."

"Good," said Mr. Smith, "but what do real mag-lev trains use? Crashing into the wooden walls would cause friction and damage."

"There are repelling and attracting magnets on the side walls as well."

Mr. Smith nodded. "And what do we call that floating on a bubble?"

"Levitation."

Mr. Smith nodded. "What's the final ingredient for a mag-lev train?"

"Propulsion," Dexter replied. He gently dropped a flat magnet at the starting point of the track. A tiny French mag-lev train constructed out of pieces of a colored index card was taped to its top side.

"Cute," said Mr. Smith, grinning.

"Seats and tray tables in the upright and locked positions," Dexter said with a smile. "No smoking please." With a gentle flick of his finger, he launched the magnet down the length of the track. "We've cleared the station," he said. The magnet glided smoothly down the four-foot length of track and stopped abruptly when it hit the towels bunched at the endpoint. "Now arriving, track number one, the Dexter Express."

Mr. Smith chuckled. "OK, Mr. Conductor, what was the propulsion mechanism with this model?"

"My finger."

"What's the propulsion mechanism in real mag-lev trains?"

Dexter thought for a moment before speaking. "There are electrified coils in the walls and track?"

Mr. Smith nodded again. "So?"

"So real mag-lev trains move because people alternate the electrical current that goes to the magnetic coils in front and back of the train," said Dexter.

"What does that change?" Mr. Smith asked

"The polarity of the magnetic coils," Dexter replied. "The ones in front attract the magnets attached underneath the train while the ones in back repel the underneath magnets at the same moment, giving it thrust. The train moves forward."

"Excellent, Dexter," Mr. Smith commended. "You nailed it. Now how about a working model of what you just described?"

"You mean make a model that has side and track magnets that alternate polarity at the same times? Using real electrical coils?"

"Yes. Small, homemade coils, but yes."

Dexter paused. "I don't know," he began. "Have any of your students ever done this in class?"

"Nope. You'll be the first," Mr. Smith replied.

"Can it be done?" Dexter asked.

"I don't know. If a working model isn't feasible, you can make a stationary one with lots of arrows showing forces. You can use it to explain the idea to the class. Either one will be fine."

Dexter looked at the floor, then back at his teacher. "When's it due?" he asked.

"End of the week," Mr. Smith replied. "Is it a deal?"

Dexter nodded and said, "Yeah," but his mind was already searching for sources for electric coils.

Dexter's model that applied what he was learning in physical science class was his summarization. After he read and listened to information on magnetic levitation trains, he built a model to explore the ideas. Such interactions result in far more learning than could be achieved by answering questions at the end of a chapter.

It's the manipulation of ideas and information that leads to learning. Cognitive theorists tell us that we must change our interaction with information in order to learn it. That means if we read it, we must talk about it, write about it, draw it, dance to it, or interact with it in a manner other than reading so we can process it. Building models provides a highly effective way to do this—not only for tactile, kinesthetic students, but for all of us.

Basic Sequence

First, consider the essential and enduring concepts, facts, and skills you're teaching. Then, identify those that could be expressed through some sort of model, even if you can't think of a specific model right now. Remember, models aren't always three-dimensional constructions; they can be drawn on paper too. Nor are they always stationary; some models only exist when objects are in motion. And although some parts of your curriculum may not seem suitable for modeling, your students will find a way to build models anyway—good ones!

Assign the model, or give your students a choice to summarize using a model. Make sure they have sufficient time and materials to plan, draw or build, and explain their models to classmates—each step is critical to this summarization technique's effectiveness.

As students work, don't hesitate to monitor them closely and to ask guiding questions. This building stage is not a time to let them fly solo; if you wait until students present completed models, you miss the prime learning window. Also be sure to display students' completed models so classmates can interact within them in a substantive manner.

Variations and Extended Applications

Imagine the summarization and interaction that would result from building models of the following principles and concepts:

- Checks and balances within the U.S. federal government
- Molecules and particular bonds
- Photosynthesis
- Levers and pulleys
- Parabolas and trajectories for missiles
- The Globe Theatre
- Cellular respiration
- Persuasive essays
- War strategies
- Population increases during times of heavy immigration and the subsequent drain on resources
- Erosion
- Pythagorean Theorem
- Pascal's triangle
- Boyle's law

- Poetic rhyming patterns

- Aristotle's rhetorical triangle

- Proportions

- Velocity = time divided by distance

- Symbolic portrayals of systems of government

- Latitude and longitude

- Terrariums of specific biomes

- Metabolism

- The immune system

- Cardiopulmonary resuscitation (CPR)

- Geometric progressions

- Sets and subsets of ideas

- Slope and y-intercept

- Computer programming, flow charts

- Conversations and human interactions

Camp Songs

Remember the old song about the green grass growin' all around a tree that was in a trunk that was in a hole in the ground? The song builds with each verse, adding progressively to the increasingly outlandish mental picture as we sing. One line runs like this: "Well, the bug on the bud, the bud on the twig, the twig on the branch, the branch on the limb, the limb on the tree, the tree in the trunk, the trunk in the hole, and the hole in the ground, and the green grass growin' all around, all around, with the green grass growin' all around. Hey!"

The song is a great mnemonic device for remembering a long list of things, and the camp song summarization technique is just what it sounds like: teaching students a few camp song melodies and asking them to compose new lyrics based on lesson content. Imagine using the green grass song to help students review and remember content such as taxonomy, a time line, a sequence of events, a lab procedure, or the elements in a particular grouping.

Basic Sequence

Have some fun. Select and teach your students a camp song from your childhood or one that you sang around a campfire at summer camp. The following songs lend themselves to lyric substitutions:

- "Green Grass Growin' All Around"
- "Lion Hunt"
- "This Old Man"
- "On Top of Old Smoky"
- "I've Been Working on the Railroad"
- "Puff, the Magic Dragon"
- "My Darling Clementine"
- "Home on the Range"

- "The Yellow Duck Song"
- "Little Bunny Foo Foo"
- "Titanic"
- "Patsy-Ory-Ory-Aye!"
- "Head, Shoulder, Knees, and Toes"
- "I Am the Musicanner"
- "Father Abraham"
- "My Aunt Came Back"
- "Boom-Chicka-Boom"

Once your students have memorized the tune, ask them to change the lyrics to reflect their new learning. Do a think-aloud demonstration to give students an idea of what it would sound like. It's also OK to write a few verses yourself to get students started. The first time you introduce the idea, you might want to write an entire song's lyrics as a whole class; generally, though, this works best as a small-group activity. Students will learn more and their "songwriting" will go faster.

Although there are artistic elements to this technique, remember that the goal isn't so much the song; it's the students' discourse while they generate the song. Noise can be a productive thing. When they are ready to present, however, ask students to review their new lyrics, making sure everything is as accurate, clear, and complete as possible.

As each group performs, invite the class to critique the song for accuracy, clarity, and completeness. If possible, share the songs by photocopying a few so the whole class can use them for studying the topics. Publish some songs in the school's literary magazine, if you can.

Variations and Extended Applications

Other song genres, plus poetry, can also work well. Even if you don't personally enjoy rap music, consider asking students to rap about course content. If rap music permeates their lives, then embrace it as a positive teaching tool. The rhythmic repetitions and content-packed nature of rap music make it very effective for learning new material. Again, remember that the students' creation of the rap, not its presentation to the class, is where the greatest learning occurs.

The blues is another form of music that works well for the classroom. Play a few blues songs in class—anything from the upbeat tempos of the Blues Brothers to the mournful laments of B. B. King singing that he's got the blues somethin' bad. As students listen, provide copies of lyrics so they get the idea of how the music is constructed. Once students "get the blues," ask them to choose a blues style to emulate as they tell the story of the week's content. Then sit back and listen to their soulful expression in the "I've got the multiplyin', mixed-number blues," or the gotta-dance beat of "Cell Man" (a cytology-themed "Soul Man").

Don't forget Dr. Seuss. Students of all ages find Seuss verses a lot of fun, and Seuss-influenced poems poking fun at grammar, computers, politicians, and more abound on the Internet. Invite students to share in the fun as they design Seuss renditions of math facts, the contributions of ancient Egypt, or of flower parts. If students need a template, have them use any Seuss story and rewrite a few pages using new lyrics but following the same structure. It doesn't matter if the meter and syllabication are off. As long as the poem has a fair attempt at rhyme and a beat in concert with accurate content, it'll work. Oh, the places you'll go!

Carousel Brainstorming

This technique gets students rising, moving, and conversing.

Basic Sequence

Around the room, post newsprint or poster board showing quotes, questions, or concepts related to the week's learning. Divide your students into groups of four to six and give each group a different color of marking pen, crayon, or pencil. Place each group in front of a poster.

In the space provided on the poster board or newsprint, have each group add its ideas about the topic written at the top. Students might list attributes of something, consider an issue and form an opinion, or compare one thing to another. No matter what the poster requests, it's requiring groups to review information about the week's learning. As each group arrives at each posting, have students consider the other groups' contributions as they also respond to the prompts.

With this technique, it's important to keep things moving. Set a time limit for responding to each poster's prompts. One to two minutes is sufficient for younger grade levels, but middle school and older students can be at one poster for five minutes or more. Groups should begin their task when you start the clock; when time is up, tell students to proceed immediately to the next poster; then start the clock again. Continue until all groups have visited all posters, then ask each group to summarize the information on one poster for the whole class.

Variations and Extended Applications

To increase challenge and accountability, ask each group to record two salient points from each poster they visit and create a written summary of all the concepts using those two points from each poster. Don't forget the artistic/structural portion of students' minds: Some topics may be best presented on these posters as mindmaps. Student groups go to each poster and add another labeled turn, arrow, symbol, or extension of the mindmap that everyone is building on that paper.

Another variation is to ask students to take a stance independently: Each one considers every prompt, then stands under the one that best represents his or her opinion or state of mind about the topic. Once students have clustered under their chosen posters, ask a few from each group to explain their position.

If it's easier, ask students to sit in small groups, and move the papers with prompts from group to group. This way, students aren't up moving around the room—which may be a positive or negative thing, depending on the situation.

Charades

Yes, the old party game has new life as a summarization experience. Students who present clues must generate the essential attributes of the concept or fact, and students who guess must analyze the performance in light of what they know. Both sides win.

Basic Sequence

Divide the class into two teams and then have students within each team choose a partner or form a small group of three or four. Distribute slips of paper identifying concepts, facts, people, and skills you've been teaching. Ask partners or small groups to discuss what they know about the topics they've received and the essential attributes of those topics. This activity is the first round of summarization. The second round occurs when they revisit their attribute lists to determine a set of pantomime motions that they can use to symbolically portray the different attributes of their assigned topics. Throughout the process, students must speak very quietly so they aren't overheard by anyone in the other groups. This may mean taking the class to another part of the building or school grounds so that the groups can spread out.

When everyone is ready, reassemble as two teams and have partners or small groups present their pantomimes to the other partners or small groups within their team. Give points if their teams can guess what they're presenting. Consider prohibiting the use of typical Charades clue motions, however, such as "sounds like," "TV," "movie," and fingers against the forearm indicating the number of syllables. Make your students create pure expressions of content for every step of the game.

Variations and Extended Applications

The familiar game of Pictionary® is a different spin on Charades. Instead of pantomiming, students draw clues for the topic. They can't use numbers, words, or gestures, nor can they talk or point to anything around them. This is usually great fun, and once my students review material this way, they always want to do it again.

Incidentally, if you want more detailed rules, official game boxes of Charades and Pictionary are available in most toy stores. However, the basic party versions we learned as children are enough for satisfying summarization experiences.

Concrete Spellings

Blending art and content can be an illuminating way to summarize. In this technique, students write key concept words "in the shape of their meaning." This idea is similar to concrete poetry, in which poems are written so that their appearance echoes the topics they address (e.g., a poem about a tree has lines that form the shape of a tree, and a poem about a pyramid has lines that form a pyramid). For concrete spellings, students spell the words using letters that form shapes to express the words' meanings (see Figure 16). If the word is "tall," the letters could be very tall on the page. If the word is "analysis," the letters could be broken into smaller pieces, showing their essential elements.

— **FIGURE 16** —
Concrete Spellings

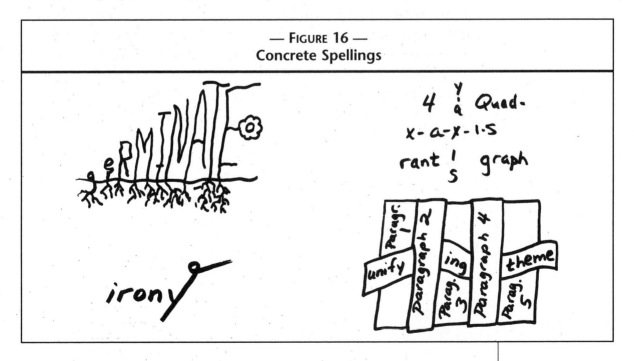

Basic Sequence

After presenting classroom content and skills to students, either identify or remind them of the essential vocabulary terms. Ask students to spell the words in a form that reveals their meanings, and be sure to show some examples: Part artwork, part cartoon, and all definition, this task can be approached in many ways. The learning occurs as students draft, revise, and generate their concept art.

Variations and Extended Applications

Although I typically assign concrete spellings as an individual activity, allowing groups of students to talk over and share ideas in small groups can be good review and can help to spark ideas.

If students are hesitant, you might want to conduct this activity as a whole class. Write a word or two on the chalkboard or an overhead transparency. Let the students brainstorm possible ways to spell those words "concretely" and then ask them to create some draft spellings. The following day, ask them to share their most innovative and well-defined concrete spellings on a piece of large mural paper, on an overhead slide, or on a bulletin board. Let the class tour the concrete spellings, observing and critiquing each other's interpretations. The conversation serves as a second summarizing experience, beyond just the genesis of the spellings.

Students take this exercise with them to other classes on their own; it's that effective and that much fun. For more inspiration on using graphics to represent vocabulary, look at *Vocabutoons* (Burchers, Burchers, & Burchers, 1996).

Design a Test

Everyone likes to play teacher once in a while. Most students enjoy this technique, especially if teachers use students' creations on the real test. Thinking of what questions and prompts a teacher might use and what successful responses would be helps students to focus on the desired outcome of their learning and can make reviewing seem like less of a chore.

This technique also opens the door to valuable in-class discussions of teaching and assessment—the kind of metacognitive examination that helps both students and teachers. Have students contemplate these questions: Why do we teach and assess the way we do? Does it work for everyone? How could we get a more accurate picture of what students know and are able to do?

Basic Sequence

Explain to your students how teachers come up with test questions. Then show effective and ineffective questions, and ask students to identify what makes the questions work. Review different types of questions, and ask students to generate a few sample questions right then. Possible question formats include multiple choice, true or false, short answer, fill-in-the-blank, matching, diagrams, short essay, analogies, and even inventing something new that incorporates the facts or concepts you're assessing through the test. Remind students to use a balance of constructed-response items (where test-takers generate information and applications on their own, e.g., short answers, essays, and fill-ins) and forced-choice items (where test-takers select a response from a set of options, e.g., multiple choice, true-false, matching).

When your students seem to have mastered the basic idea of successful assessment prompts, ask them to design two test questions and to share them with a classmate for critiquing. The students should discuss both what the questions are and what successful responses should include. By trying to respond to their own questions, students see the questions' weak points; they can throw them out or revise them accordingly.

When students have two solid questions and responses, ask them to create a well-crafted quiz or test for the subject they're learning. Invite them to use various prompts and formats, some traditional and some innovative. You might even suggest that for any well-stated question that you decide to use on the real test, the author of that question will get bonus points on the test.

Variations and Extended Applications

There's lots of leeway as you apply this technique. Will you make your students answer their own test questions, answer a classmate's test questions, or answer only a few of their own as they review? Will they have to answer in writing as if they were taking the test, or do they just have to go over the answers orally with a classmate?

Different situations dictate different decisions. In my experience, though, students are hesitant to create the kind of complex questions that require elaborate written responses if they believe they'll need to answer those questions themselves. It's often better to ask students to chose a partner and review each other's questions. They can discuss the correct responses, but need only write suggestions for improving the questions.

Every time I use this technique with students, they create wonderful questions. I've also found that they achieve a sense of ownership of the test and take it more seriously, regardless of their grade level or the subject. Some students really get into the experience of matching questions to the learning as they make sure questions are thoughtful and discuss the lessons' content. I can't help but think of the seeds being planted to grow future teachers.

Exclusion Brainstorming

Students like this technique because it's like playing detective and searching for patterns in a crime. You can even let it get competitive if you want. The important part for learning is the students' rationales for their answers to which word doesn't belong. Emphasize that part of the experience.

Basic Sequence

Write the topic on an overhead slide or chalkboard, followed by a series of words (or short phrases), all but one of which connects to or "fits with" the topic. You could also do this on paper in advance, and distribute copies so that every student has one. The task for students is to draw a line through the word that does not connect with the topic and to circle those words that do. Then the "brainstormer" needs to explain why the circled words are connected to the topic and why the crossed-out word is not. Figure 17 shows how a student might mark a prompt in science class.

— FIGURE 17 —
Exclusion Brainstorming

Mixtures: plural, separable, ~~dissolves~~, no formula

Compounds: chemically combined, new properties, has formula, ~~no composition~~

Solutions: ~~heterogeneous mixture~~, dissolved particles, saturated and unsaturated, heat increases

Suspensions: ~~clear~~, no dissolving, settles upon standing, larger than molecules

You might schedule this activity before the lesson or after, depending on whether you're pre-assessing or assessing. They key is to be purposeful in your choice of words. Always include the ones that compel students to consider the concepts and relationships you want them to learn.

Variations and Extended Applications

This technique is easy to adapt for varied readiness levels. Choose words that have very subtle connections to the topic or very overt ones, depending on students' needs. The connections can be in terms of analogies, such as making all the words or phrases synonyms, antonyms, subsets, examples of, categories for, indicators of rising intensity, or indicators of decreasing intensity.

The Frayer Model

The Frayer Model has been around for more than three decades and was recently described in *Classroom Instruction That Works* (Marzano, Pickering, & Pollock, 2001). Figure 18 shows the set-up.

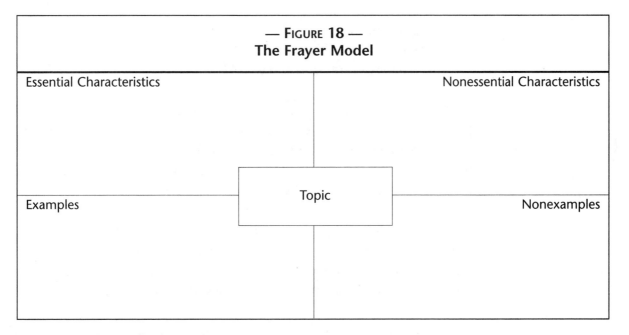

— FIGURE 18 —
The Frayer Model

Essential Characteristics

Nonessential Characteristics

Topic

Examples

Nonexamples

Basic Sequence

In the center of the Frayer Model graphic organizer, have your students record a topic to be summarized. In the upper left corner, they should list attributes of the topic that are pertinent and essential to the unit of study. This is the critical definition for students to learn. For instance, if the topic were "cumulonimbus cloud formations," students would list essential characteristics such as "large, usually shaped like anvils, build to great heights."

In the nonessential characteristics box, they should write "made of water droplets, white, gray, sometimes foretell difficult weather ahead." Although the attributes are interesting, they're less important to understanding the topic. Allow explanatory diagrams in any of the boxes as appropriate.

In the boxes on the lower half of the Frayer Model, students should draw properly formed cumulonimbus clouds on the left and noncumulonimbus cloud formations on the right. Depending on the topic and the students' developmental levels, you could ask students to draw nonexamples that are subtly different from the examples and then ask them to explain in short captions what those differences are. For example, when studying similes, students could write the same thing on both sides, but underline the inclusion of "like" or "as."

> *Topic:* Similes
> *Example:* "Life is like a wheel."
> *Nonexample:* "His life was a wheel."

Notice I didn't indicate what the nonexample was (a metaphor). It just says, "nonexample." Everything in the model is expressed in terms of being or not being a simile. Our minds tend to store new information by how it's similar to what's already in mental storage, not how it's different. If I introduced the label for the nonexamples, "metaphor" in this case, students might confuse the topic with its nonexamples. To prevent confusion or inaccurate extrapolation, everything in the Frayer Model summarization should be expressed in terms of the topic written in the center square. Try not to introduce commonly confused vocabulary terms in the nonexamples or nonessential characteristics boxes.

Variations and Extended Applications

Although the model suggests using visual responses such as drawings, consider asking your students to respond using other modes and media. For example, the Frayer Model can be vividly portrayed on a student-constructed Web site, in a short video, or in a library or classroom display. Students can also express examples and nonexamples, or essential and nonessential characteristics, in a public speech or character monologue in a play. How about the essentials and nonessentials of something via a musical piece? If your class is ready for it, how about expressing the four categories through sculpting with modeling clay?

Human Bingo

This technique combines a familiar game format with demonstration of content mastery and is a universal favorite across grade levels and disciplines. It's like an accordion that a teacher can expand or contract according to class size and content needs.

Basic Sequence

Make sure you have the following items: bingo cards with categories written in the squares (see Figure 19); edible game markers (see notes on this in a moment); pens or pencils; students' names written on individual pieces of paper; and a small box, bowl, or hat from which to draw names.

Provide each student with a bingo card—a five-by-five grid with 25 spaces. Make sure the center space is labeled "Free." In each of the other 24 spaces, list a content component you want students to review, plus a few fun things just to add interest. For example, a math teacher could put math problems or terms in each of the spaces, English teachers could use grammar terms or concepts for the novel under study, and science teachers could use terms or lab protocols. Some fun additions might be to insert phrases such as "has seen [insert the name of the latest popular movie]," "plays basketball," "has traveled more than 500 miles away," or "is under six feet tall."

Give your students about 8 to 10 minutes to move about the room getting their classmates to sign the squares on their bingo card. The card's owner signs the free space. A classmate may sign a square only if he or she can do, solve, or successfully respond to the prompt on that square. In some classes, you may let the card owner sign one other square—if that helps.

— FIGURE 19 —
Human Bingo

Can make a strange noise with his or her body	Can make into a polynomial: $(x + 1)(x + 3)$	Can demonstrate titration	Can solve: $2/3 - 1^4/5$	Knows two products of photosynthesis
Can define "_____"	Knows three causes for the Civil War	Knows the capitals of the countries of South America	Knows three conflicts in *No Promises in the Wind*	Knows four main stages of mitosis
Can import a picture from Internet and can insert it into a report	Can perform three approved gymnastic moves	*FREE SPACE*	Knows four basic passes in basketball	Personal pronoun, 3rd person objective, plural
Can sing part of any song by Creedence Clearwater Revival	Knows the difference between meiosis and mitosis	Knows six things to consider when making difficult decisions	Knows the differences between squid and octopus	Knows formula for area of a triangle
Knows what comes next: J, F, M, A, M, _?_	Can name 24 bones with the proper terms	Can draw the sequence of energy transfer in ecosystems	Can perform "_____"	Can list three differences between WWI and WWII

After all squares are filled with signatures, everyone sits down, and you call names drawn from a container. If that name appears on their cards, students place a sunflower seed, M&M, piece of popcorn, animal cracker, or something else edible on the square. Why make the markers edible? It adds to the enjoyment. If someone else earns a bingo, it's not so bad—everyone gets to eat their markers. Try not use peanuts because of the rise of peanut allergies in today's students.

The first student to get five in a row yells, "Human Bingo!" Ask the student to name each square's prompt, as well as the student who said he or she could respond to that prompt. As names are called, the students who signed those squares must demonstrate their ability to do what they said they could do: solve the problem, respond to the prompt, and so on. If all five students demonstrate everything successfully, declare it a successful bingo, and let the class eat the markers placed on their boards. If one or more of the five students in the row can't demonstrate an accurate response, then no bingo is awarded and the game continues.

Motivated to keep the game going (and to win themselves), the rest of the class listens critically during the demonstrations, making sure that each student's response is accurate and comprehensive. By evaluating classmates' responses, they are reviewing content and skills for themselves.

Variations and Extended Applications

Some other versions of bingo include "picture frame," in which everyone tries to fill the outer perimeter of squares, and "blackout," in which everyone tries to fill in all squares. If your class is small or your time is short, use a three-by-three grid instead of a five-by-five grid ("Bin!" instead of "Bingo!") or allow your students to sign their names to more than one space. When you first teach and play the game, give the activity 30 minutes or more. After that initial time, however, you can play Human Bingo as a review game or summarization strategy in 20 minutes or less.

Human Continuum

In this technique, also known as a mobile Socratic seminar, students put their bodies where their minds are. They're getting up, moving, arguing, justifying, and learning. And it all starts with just a line on the floor and a few questions from you.

When students stand along a continuum, they carry their notes, notebooks, articles, and anything else they need to justify their opinions and bolster their responses to your questions. Providing evidence for one's claim is a scholarly skill that, in conjunction with the conversation, gives this activity its Socratic seminar feel. (See page 140 for a detailed discussion of the Socratic seminar summarization technique.)

Basic Sequence

Place a line on the floor (using masking or carpet tape) or on the ceiling (using thick yarn). Because you are creating a line and not a line segment, place arrows on both ends so it resembles a continuum. Place a large "A," for "agree," just past the arrow on one side and a large "D," for "disagree," just past the arrow on the other side. At the approximate midpoint of the continuum, place a piece of tape or yarn perpendicular to the longer line. This position represents the "I don't know" or "I'm not comfortable sharing what I know" zone.

The line must be a minimum of 30 feet so it can accommodate students' bodies. Make it longer if you can. If you don't have a long straight space for such a line-up, don't worry. For years, my lines have wound among desks and tables in my classroom. As long as I have an "A" end, a "D" end, and a midpoint, it works fine. Or you can create the line outside your classroom. It works well in the front lobby of the school, on a sidewalk, in a hallway, in the gym, in the cafeteria, or even in the parking lot where you've set up traffic cones to block traffic. Our classroom walls are merely suggestions.

After establishing the line, use it. The human continuum can be done at any point in the lesson: as a pre-assessment or way to prime the mind, as a mid-unit check of comprehension, or as a way to process what has been learned and to assess comprehension at the end of a unit. Let's assume your students have just completed a unit of study, and you're helping them pull it all together.

If space is short, identify a subset of students to represent the whole class. If you have plenty of space, create two or more lines in the classroom, and divide the class among the multiple lines. Thus, everyone participates, instead of just a dozen students while the rest sit passively. Ask students to choose positions along the line and to stand there; it doesn't matter where they stand as you begin.

To start, make a statement to the students about something they've been studying. Then ask students to move their bodies' locations along the continuum to indicate they agree or disagree with the statement. If they only sort of agree with something, they can move just a little along the line toward the "A," not all the way. The same holds for the disagree side. If they don't understand, are confused, or are not comfortable in responding, those students should stand at the midpoint of the continuum (at the perpendicular line).

"All trapezoids are quadrilaterals," you say. Students must consider the key points—"all," "trapezoid," "quadrilateral"—and then must move. Give them about 30 seconds to get into position. Anything can happen, of course: they can all be gathered at one end or in the middle, they can be fairly evenly spread, or they can be lopsidedly spread with all but two students on one side. Regardless of the distribution, you can use it for a teachable moment.

After each statement and the students' repositioning, call on one or two students at several locations to justify their positions. If they need to leave the line for a moment to go to the chalkboard or to get something to help explain their thinking, let them. If you have students at both ends of the continuum, ask them to give points and counterpoints in their rationale. For those in the middle, ask one or two to explain their confusion. Ask those who are only partially toward "A" or "D" to explain their hesitation or to tell what it would take to move them fully one way or the other.

In the next step, ask students to adjust their positions after hearing their classmates' reasoning. The inclination to revise one's thinking in light of new evidence is a sign of an intellect. Let students re-adjust. Remember, too, that students hear and elevate in importance the content that comes from classmates. However, you must make sure that nothing inaccurate is communicated. If you think students are concluding something incorrect, you must increase your probing questions as you ask them to justify their position.

What do you do with students who always follow the supposed "smart" kids? Ask those students to defend their positions. If you already have a culture of randomly calling on students to justify their points of view, everyone will know that they can't be correct merely by association with the perceived "brainiacs." They'll learn quickly that it's acceptable, even preferred, to stand in the "I don't know" zone when they truly don't know.

Another advantage of this technique is that it helps you to identify the students standing at the midpoint, in the "I don't know" zone. A quick glance shows you whom you need to reteach. Record the names of these students, the concepts, and the date on a sticky note, then put it in your planning book for a mini-lesson tomorrow. If more than half the class stands in the "I don't know" zone, you might consider reteaching the whole lesson in a different way. If you do reteach the whole lesson, then the mini-lessons would be for students who are standing at the end indicating the correct response. They will need a differentiated lesson to take them to the next level.

Variations and Extended Applications

Here is an example of two statements. Both are from science, but one is a fact and the other is an opinion.

"Biodiversity has little effect on temperate biomes."

"The good that comes from genetic engineering of humans out-weighs the bad."

The first example asks students to consider its logic. If they agree, then they are saying that biodiversity has little effect; if they disagree, they are saying that biodiversity has a great effect. Students must prepare for such discussions and must bring along evidence to support their statements.

In the second example, ask your students to express an opinion. They still must have concrete evidence for why they believe as they do and must use it in their discussions. In addition to using their notes, notebooks, and articles, are they allowed to share personal religious beliefs? Sure. Those beliefs are a part of their world. You're not indoctrinating them into any one faith. Instead, you invite any element they might use to form a thoughtful response. It can be very powerful for students to hear their classmates' thinking.

By the way, I've had a student stand at the midpoint and leap from side to side while waiting for the discussion and next question. When I saw this, my first inclination was to speak harshly, "Manny! Stop dancing back and forth like that and follow the rules, or you'll be asked to sit down!" I discarded that response, however, and instead asked him what he was trying to express. I thought it might be indecision. I was wrong.

"I can see both sides," Manny explained. "In some situations, I disagree, and in some situations, I agree."

Although Manny technically broke the rules by not choosing one side or the other, I wasn't going to admonish him. This was a time for affirmation. Manny's was the most intellectual response a student had made all day. Very few situations are purely black and white. It takes a real thinker to see the gray areas and occasionally decide to break with protocols to explore other ideas. Manny is going to be a successful citizen with thinking like that. I praised him and continued the discussion.

In another example, the students are presented with these sentences related to their reading of Erich Remarque's *All Quiet on the Western Front*:

"Cruel trainers make the most useful trainers for soldiers about to go to war."

"According to the author, Remarque, cruel trainers make the most useful trainers for soldiers about to go to war."

Students should position themselves along the line to reflect their beliefs and should have copies of the book with sticky notes highlighting excerpts that provide evidence for their rationale. No matter which way they respond, they must justify their stance using substantive passages from the text. Look at each example prompt, however. The second prompt says, "According to the author"; the first one does not. In the first, the situation is threatening to students because it asks what they think personally. In the second, the situation is not so threatening because it asks students to report what the author thinks. Nonthreatening situations tend to support more risk-taking, even from introverts. It's safe to report what others think; we become vulnerable when we share our personal thoughts. Consider how you frame your questions. In some cases, your frame will liberate students' thinking; in other cases, it will shackle thinking.

I've also used this activity with adults, such as when faculty members are considering a new pedagogy, master schedule, or homogeneity versus heterogeneity in math classes. It works just as well. You can even use it for character education with students, as in the following example:

"It's OK to tell little white lies once in a while in order to protect a person's feelings."

"It's not cheating to copy someone else's homework when we already understand the concept. We don't need the practice the teacher thought we did."

Versatile and substantive, the human continuum is a popular activity with both students and teachers. It's one more way to meet the needs of innately social brains. It also gets students out of their seats, relieving stresses on bone growth plates, stretching their muscles, and allowing them to converse thoughtfully in a standing position—something not often done in schools yet worth learning how to do. After all, your students and mine will need good preparation for all their debates in the U.S. Congress, in the United Nations, and over the backyard fence with their neighbors.

Inner or Outer Circle

This activity is common in church youth groups and adult professional meetings, but it works with all levels and subjects in schools. It's also another way to get folks out of their seats and moving around the room. The movement increases blood flow to the brain—always a positive thing for both students and teachers.

Basic Sequence

Ask half your class to stand in a large circle, facing into the circle, with about a body width (two to three feet) in between each person. If your classroom can't accommodate a circle this size, take the students somewhere inside or outside the building that can. Ask the other half of the class to form a circle in the center of the first circle with each student facing someone in the outer circle. Each pair of students should be conversationally close, again about two to three feet. If done properly, this arrangement creates an inner and outer circle, the outer circle facing the center and the inner one facing out.

Think of the two circles as gears, one moving outside the other. Choose one of the gears to remain in position while the other one moves, at least at first. Later you can add movement to the other gear. For this example, we'll keep the inside gear in position and move only the outer gear.

In this first position, ask facing partners to each answer a review question about the most recent learning. If possible, make it something that has more than one possible response, such as "Why did the South secede from the Union?" or "How does gravity help planets maintain their orbits?" instead of one-word response questions such as "Who wrote *The Lord of the Flies*?" Give students 30 seconds apiece or a total of one minute for both students to respond. Allow shorter or longer response times, according to the unique needs of your students.

When time is up, ask the outer gear or circle of students to move a particular number of people to the right or left. Keep track of where you send folks so you don't repeat partnerships, if possible. Once the students are in new positions, ask the new partners another review question and repeat the procedure. Continue the activity for anywhere from 10 to 20 minutes, then ask the students to resume their seats. Spend a few moments debriefing what they heard and felt.

One added benefit from this activity is it provides a way for students who don't normally talk with one another to interact. It's not embarrassing unless they didn't do their homework or participate in the earlier learning. Even then, such students can be invited to ask probing questions of the other students' responses until time is called.

Variations and Extended Applications

As a variation, first, split your class in half, or for variety put boys against girls (the number can be uneven). Give each member of one group a letter; give the members of the other a number. Then have one group form the inside circle and the other the outside circle. The circles will move in opposite directions.

Call out a letter and a number—as a pair—and ask a question. The person who answers correctly first remains in his or her circle. The other person leaves the circle. You don't have to eliminate people, but it gives the "game" a different feeling. If you do remove people, make sure you remove their corresponding letter or number.

Also, if you don't have room in your classroom to form circles or if you can't relocate, this variation can be done with your students remaining in their seats.

Jigsaws

Remember John Godfrey Saxe's famous poem in which six blind men from Indostan come upon an elephant? They each touch a different portion of the elephant and quickly judge what makes an elephant, drawing only on the portion they touch. The one who touches an ear, for example, thinks an elephant is a fan. The one who touches a leg thinks an elephant is a tree. The one who touches the trunk thinks an elephant is a snake. The reader understands that if the men collaborated and put their pieces of the puzzle together, they would have a more accurate definition of an elephant.

Jigsaw activities work the same way. They do three things for students: help students rely on each other in a collaborative task, show students how to find the truth, and show students how to divide a task into manageable chunks. If the task is to understand a historical event, a country, a person, or a math or science concept, students each take a smaller chunk of the larger topic, study and summarize it, and then teach it to the rest of their study group. Once each has shared his or her piece of the whole truth about a topic, all students will have the full picture and will be closer to the truth.

With this technique, students can learn complicated material without having to take on an enormous amount of individual investigation. They must trust their classmates to summarize accurately, of course, but such study groups have a commitment to one another. As teachers, we can monitor that commitment.

Basic Sequence

Present the major topic to be learned by the small group. This topic can be the same for every group, or different groups can have different topics.

Help your groups identify the subtopics within the main topic, or tell them what their subtopics will be, again according to their needs. For example, if the topic is Germany, groups might identify these subtopics to study: culture, geography, industry, monetary system, and political system. Each student will take one subtopic and study it, then will prepare a well-crafted summary of the material to bring back to the group. Students may do this task over several days or weeks, or the task might be limited to reading and digesting short sections of the textbook within the class period.

If time allows when students are ready to share their piece of the puzzle with the group, ask them to have something written and something visual to share. The group members then share their pieces of the puzzle with their group.

To keep groups focused on the task, consider having them create a product that allows them to demonstrate what they learned in the jigsaw activity. The product can take many forms, including a completed matrix or graphic organizer, a short summary of a few facts from each area, a small group artwork that expresses accurate information about each subtopic, or a learning log entry or two in which students respond to what was shared by their group. Invite group members to ask one another questions during the presentation. Remember that the presenting student has become a mini-expert on the subtopic within that group.

Variations and Extended Applications

Jigsaw activities make great cooperative learning experiences, but you shouldn't limit their use only to times when you're doing formal cooperative learning in your classes. This summarizing technique appeals to the social interaction needs of the mind. Each student becomes a teacher, and the workload is divided for conquering.

Learning Logs and Journals

Sometimes your greater gift to your students is to provide an initial core of knowledge, but then to show them that isn't all there is—that knowledge is fluid, subject to context, time, and imagination. Learning is more of a process than a product. By asking students to maintain a log or journal of their learning experiences and reflections, you can enable them to make the best of the learning process. Such strategies are key to helping some students become lifelong learners. Learning logs and journals also provide an intimate look at students' thinking and help students monitor their own understanding.

I regularly use the terms "log" and "journal" interchangeably because both describe the strategy of asking students to record facts, observations, and concepts in a notebook or other medium and to comment and reflect on that material in the same medium. Students don't have to use a notebook, however; PDAs, computer logs, tape recorders, CDs, videos, and other forms are all possible alternatives to a traditional, written journal.

Basic Sequence

Although there are many ways to set up a journal, all require multiple entries over several days or weeks. The first step in using journals is to provide a learning experience and ask students to record the essence of it in their journals. The journal entry might be in the form of notes on a lecture, a recording of math problems and their proper solutions, a diagram of Newton's laws of motion, a list of the unique characteristics of Jeffersonian economics. The important thing is for students to record the factual information in their journals so that it is readily accessible.

Next, provide students with a prompt or choice of prompts to which they can personally respond. Try to design prompts that ask students to consider the factual information they've just recorded in a new and thoughtful manner. Here's an example of a prompt we might give to a class that has just read and taken notes on McCarthyism in the 1950s:

> "What were the elements of life in the United States in the 1950s that enabled such widespread public acceptance of McCarthyism? Do those elements exist today? If so, where and how, and what can be done about them?"

Note that the question isn't a simple, "What was McCarthyism?" Students must use their knowledge of McCarthyism and the era under study to form a response. Ask students to record the prompt in the journals, then respond below in as straightforward a manner as they can. Bulleted phrases are fine. Mechanics, punctuation, and polish should be secondary concerns.

Creating the content record and the personal response is one point of summarization and learning. The second and sometimes more effective point is having students discuss their responses with others. When students share in this way, they can see how they are doing relative to classmates and can pick up on any misconceptions they have developed. Students do best when they respond independently and then discuss their responses with partners or small groups before discussing with the whole class.

After the discussions, invite students to go back and clarify or revise their journal entries in light of what they've now learned. When you first present the idea of revising one's thinking in light of new evidence, model it several times using think-aloud experiences to show them that, yes, learning is fluid.

Variations and Extended Applications

Vary the degree of challenge through your choice of prompts. Also consider varying the response format. You might ask students to respond with a political cartoon, cartoon strip, a piece of satire, or a pretend newscast script that expresses the same ideas.

Lineup

This summarization technique, which involves students arranging themselves in a line according to a set of criteria, can be a fascinating experience. It almost always yields unanticipated yet positive results, as it illuminates both students' misconceptions and valid connections that the teacher may have missed. It also allows students to hear how their classmates are thinking about the material and it gets them moving and interacting substantively with the topic—all winning combinations.

Here's what lineup looks like. In an elementary or middle school math class, the teacher explains to a group of 10 students that they will need to line up shoulder to shoulder according to assigned mathematical values. The person given the smallest value will stand at the far left end of the line and the one with the largest value, at the far right. They're told that their classmates will critique the result. Then, the teacher passes out the value cards: $2/3$, 0.01, $4/3$, 0.00999, $1/4$, 0.67, $7/8$, 0.875, $3 5/4$, and π. The different numbers formats necessitate some serious thinking and talking:

> *Michael:* Zack, your 0.00999 is smaller than my 0.01. You have to stand on my left.
> *Zack:* . . . but 999 is bigger than 1. How can I be smaller?
> *Keisha:* [taking Zack's 0.00999 card and placing it above Michael's 0.01 card so the decimals are aligned vertically] Look, once you line up the decimals, you have 0.01 on top and 0.00999 on the bottom.
> *Zack:* Yeah, I know. One hundredth, and 999 hundred-thousandths. The 999 still seems bigger.
> *Michael:* You can't compare them like that. We're on the other side of the decimal point. They have to end in the same place value.

Megan: [pointing to the card with 0.01 on it] Oh, OK! See, fill in the zeroes after the one so you can compare them. Now you have 1,000 hundred-thousandths over 999 hundred-thousandths. Which one is bigger?

Zack: [pausing, then grinning and taking his place in line] I knew that!

Basic Sequence

Tell your students that they'll be summarizing a lesson by lining up according to criteria you'll provide. Give each student a large index card with specific information written on one side. After they've seen the information, ask them to hold the card toward the audience as they determine where to stand in the line. As they're lining up, students can discuss the relationship of everyone's position, pose questions, disagree, explain rationales, and do anything else that enables the group to come to a consensus. The goal is to be 100 percent accurate, and the students can use each other to achieve it.

The criteria for lining up can be anything, but it should be purposeful. For example, the numbers used in the opening example were based on relationships the teacher wanted to explore with students. She had noticed misconceptions in their homework assignments and areas for improvement on their test responses, so she chose numbers that would enable her to address those concerns.

The lineup groups can be anywhere from 5 to 35 students, but I recommend 6 to 10 for most activities—enough to support thorough discussions, but not so many that you can't debrief each student about his or her position in the line.

While members of one group are determining their lineup, what are the rest of the students doing? Shouting advice to classmates? Contemplating the lunch menu? Climbing the walls? None of those, we hope. Teachers want to the maximize participation of all students, not just a subset. Go ahead and make three sets of cards; then divide the class into three groups. One group can line up at the back of the room, one down the middle, and one across the front. You can take the whole class to the gym, cafeteria, front lobby, hallway, or parking lot and can have the groups line up there. If there's more than one group, there's an added motivation: Not only do they want to be accurate, but they also want to be first!

If you use multiple groups, have the groups critique each other. The first group will critique the second group, the second group will critique the third, and the third will critique the first group. For a competitive angle, give groups points for successfully identifying errors in other groups' lineups and for successfully defending their positioning against another group's assessment. The number of errors is less important than students' substantive interaction and summarization of their learning.

If you feel you can handle only one group at a time, make sure to provide something for the rest of the class to do that parallels what the lineup group is doing. For example, you might record the same numeric values on small pieces of paper and have students work in desk clusters to arrange the values in proper sequence before the lineup group finishes.

Summarization will occur at several points. The first point is when students are talking with one another as they get into position. The second point is when the students give their rationale for why they're standing in those positions. As teachers, we play Socrates, facilitator, or devil's advocate to get students to explain their rationale. Let's go back to the example scenario:

Teacher: [pointing to two students standing next to each other in the lineup] You're $1/4$ and you're 0.1. How did you two know where to stand in the sequence?

Laura: Well, I just changed my $1/4$ to a decimal. It's 0.25.

Teacher: Explain how you did that.

Laura: I just know that $1/4$ is 0.25.

Teacher: How?

Laura: Um, well, I just did four divided by one.

Keisha: You mean one divided by four, top divided by bottom.

Laura: Yeah, one divided by four. I got 0.25.

Teacher: So now what are you comparing?

Laura: 0.25 and 0.1.

Teacher: And 0.1 is what, if you add a zero to make the place values the same for comparison?

Laura: 0.10.

Teacher: So now you're comparing what?

Laura: Comparing 0.10 and 0.25. And 0.25 is bigger than 0.10, so that's why I'm standing on this side of Keisha.

Teacher: Excellent. Keisha, is there any other way to do this?

Keisha: Turn it into money.

Teacher: How does that work for us?

Keisha: $1/4$ is a quarter of a dollar, or 25 cents.

Teacher: What is that as a decimal?

Keisha: 0.25.

Teacher: So now what?

Keisha: Laura's number is 0.10, or 10 cents, and 25 cents is more than 10 cents.

Teacher: The rest of you in this line, do you accept this reasoning? [The students nod.] All right. Is there another way to do this, Craig?

Craig: Change 0.1 to a fraction and compare the fractions.

Teacher: What would 0.1 be as a fraction?

Craig: It would be $1/10$.

Teacher: Good. What would you have to determine before you could compare the fractions in that situation, Maggie?

Maggie: A least common denominator?

Teacher: Well done. [The teacher turns to whole line.] Are all three of these ways mathematically sound?

[The students nod.]

Teacher: Is there often more than one way to solve a math problem? [The students nod again.] Good. There's hope for all of us then, me included. Let's continue. . . .

There are several important aspects to note here. First, the students are doing most of the talking. It's frustrating but real: If students hear information from classmates, they tend to remember it better than if they hear the same thing from teachers. Do whatever you can to get students talking substantively with one another about the topic. Second, purposefully choose your theme for a lineup experience. The lineup should manifest relationships, concepts, and skills you want to address with students. Third, be open to new ways of thinking. I've had students stand right behind one another to express equalities, and I've had students open two different civics books with pages turned to different political ideologies and stand on each book "with one foot in each camp." Asking students to do innovative summarization activities often ends with teachers humbled in the presence of greatness.

Variations and Extended Applications

Lineup summarization can be used across many disciplines. Students could line up according to the chromatic scale; taxonomy (kingdom, phylum, class, order, family, genus, and species); proper steps in a math algorithm; Fibonacci sequence; and the proper components of a well-constructed essay. Students can line up to show categories, such as three world leaders and three unique characteristics for each leader; different types of chemical bonds and two molecules representing each of those bonds; parts of speech and three examples of those parts of speech; and characteristics of different types of logic, such as induction, deduction, Boolean logic, and computer programming flow charts.

Students can also line up according to alternating patterns: pairs of synonyms or antonyms, alkaline and nonalkaline compounds, transitive and intransitive verbs, primary and secondary colors, irrational and rational numbers, prime and composite numbers, and samples of assonance and consonance. Cycles make great patterns too. Just "unhitch" one portion of the cycle and lay it out as a linear sequence instead of a circle, or have students form a circle instead of a line. Imagine doing this technique with the energy transfer cycle (producer, first-order consumer, second-order consumer, third-order consumer, scavenger, decomposer, back to producer); the Kreb cycle; ecological succession; or phases of the moon.

Is this the end of the activity—having students line up and defend their positions? Not always. It can be, if you wish, because much has already been achieved. However, I've found that the lessons really hit home when students are asked to choose any two pairings between elements in the lineup and to explain why the elements were positioned as they were. Writing reveals misconceptions and illuminates ideas that oral discourse can't always achieve. It can be a powerful third point of summarization in the lineup technique.

Luck of the Draw

This technique tends to raise students' anxiety levels, but it keeps them focused and summarizing. I first learned about it from Jon Saphier and the trainers at Research for Better Teaching in Carlisle, Massachusetts.

Basic Sequence

Each day, students prepare a written summarization of what's been covered in class or in their reading. Then, the next day, the teacher pulls one name from a hat and that lucky student must read his or her summarization from the previous day's lesson. The rest of class critiques the summarization, with the student summarizer facilitating the discussion.

Variations and Extended Applications

If some students are uncomfortable speaking in front of the class, you may prefer to use this technique later in the school year, after they're more comfortable with their classmates or after you have had time to coach them through their fears. You might have shy students' summarizations read aloud by classmates or photocopy their summaries and pass them around. Another option is to regularly incorporate a "guest reader"—a student chosen at random to read the drawn summary—and to omit the names of the reluctant public speakers from the "readers pool" until you've addressed their difficulties or fears.

Moving Summarizations

Just think about how much we'd learn if it were possible to crawl inside a car's engine (or the human circulatory system or a molecular bond) and have a look around. Kinesthetic and tactile students would have a field day if they could physically manipulate literary devices or create a drum-line that performs an interpretation of feudal society. The moving summarization technique involves brings bringing content ideas to life through physical movement.

Basic Sequence

The idea is to use the moving body to illustrate understandings of content. If your students are reviewing a time line, for example, ask them to come up with a hand-and-arm movement for each component. The following time line would offer some great movements when rehearsed, and it would yield an accurate recital of content.

> 1754—French and Indian War starts
> 1763—Britain defeats France in French and Indian War
> 1765—British Stamp Act tax imposed on colonies
> 1775—Revolutionary War begins
> 1776—Declaration of Independence signed by Second Continental Congress
> 1781—British surrender at Yorktown
> 1787—U.S. Constitution signed
> 1789—George Washington becomes first president

What movements can we imagine? The possibilities include jamming the knuckles of a closed fist into an open palm for the Stamp Act, followed by hands making begging or "gimme-gimme" motions to symbolize the taxes imposed; a pantomime of a pen scratching across parchment (the palm of one hand) to symbolize the signing of the Declaration; and students with hands above their heads, palms forward, to symbolize the surrender of the British. For the French and Indian War, all you need is two hands symbolically crashing into each other. Your students will easily find other movements. This activity isn't necessarily silent. Students might memorize the final two digits of each year ('50, '63, '65) like football players' jersey numbers and call them out while performing the movements.

With this technique, the summarization occurs as students develop movements. Repeated demonstrations of the physical movements and content become repeated summarizations. One of the best parts is that students can review content anywhere they happen to be. They don't need books or notes when the content is connected to their bodies, and as with body analogies (see page 64), study sessions make for very amusing viewing.

Variations and Extended Applications

There are endless ways to apply this technique. For an English class example, consider Victor Borge's entertaining sound effects for punctuation marks in sentences. We can do the same—but on a larger scale—with our curriculum. Each punctuation mark can be a physical movement. Bending over or bending an elbow, twisting, or throwing both hands into the air above our heads can substitute for commas, question marks, and quotation marks, respectively. A period can be a punch into the air, and an exclamation mark can be one jump straight up. Ask students to read aloud a dialogue between two characters. Instead of literally saying the punctuation, they could make movements whenever they reach a punctuation mark. With all their punctuation marks, divided quotes are particularly fun to express.

Another variation I like is using "finger plays" to demonstrate processes. Chromosome behavior in mitosis, for example, can easily be displayed (and remembered) by moving fingers together and apart. Consider the following illustration:

1. *Prophase*—Hold your hands chest high. Let your fingers play over and around each other the way kids swim in a pool. Have your fingers

intermingle—mixing, tangling, and untangling—to show the cells are getting ready to separate.

2. *Metaphase*—The lifeguard blows the whistle for a rest period, and everyone lines up along the median (central axis). For this, turn your hands so the fingertips of one hand are touching the fingertips of the other, palms facing your chest. Slide your fingertips an inch inward, overlapping with the other fingers for effect.

3. *Anaphase*—Now the division occurs. The lifeguard asks everyone to leave the pool. It's the end of the swimming day. Slowly pull your hands away from each other, bent wrists first. While you pull them apart, one hand (Ana) says, "Goodbye, Gene," (chromosome pun intended), and the other hand (Gene) says in a deep male voice, "Goodbye, Ana." (Teachers and students can do a lot with puns here, such as saying Ana and Gene are swimming in the gene pool.) Continue separating your hands until they are a little past shoulder-width apart.

4. *Telophase*—Have your Ana hand talk to your Gene hand saying, "I'll call you on the telophase-phone." Pull your fingers and hands almost completely into separate entities, as in real mitosis. They should be farther away from each other, with your arms almost completely outstretched. The next step in mitosis is the formation of two new daughter cells, but that would require a "parent's permission slip" for most grade levels, so we won't go there.

After leading the class through a summary like this, give students time to play with the process and finger plays by going back and forth trying to keep up with a narrator. The whole process is easily remembered using the acronym PMAT, for prophase, metaphase, anaphase, and telophase. You can add other phases, such as interphase, as your students get used to the finger play summarization device.

Teachers with the right resources can also build massive organizers for their students. For example, with colored chalk, draw or have students draw a huge interior diagram of the heart on the blacktop or front sidewalk. Then teach your students how blood flows from the body back into the heart, through the chambers and valves, to the lungs, back to the heart, through more chambers and valves, then out to the body again as you have them walk through the sequence on the chalk diagram. Students can narrate the specific process while doing it. Partners can move through the heart, one student reading from a script, the other one holding purple construction paper for unoxygenated blood visiting the lungs, red construction paper for oxygenated blood after. The pair can do crazy movements or dances in the lung area to simulate the oxygen–carbon dioxide exchange. Afterward, ask the students to return to their seats and read the textbook chapter on blood flow through the heart; then to accurately draw, color, and label the heart and blood flowing through it. For having experienced immersion in a heart organizer, students' minds are primed for successful retrieval from the textbook chapter.

One final example: A few years ago, I had just finished teaching the basic writing process—prewriting, drafting, revising, editing, and publishing—and all its permutations. To help students summarize what they learned, I tempted fate by distributing modeling clay. Then I told everyone to sculpt something intricate and to describe what they were doing using only terms related to the writing process.

The results were amazing. When the students made indentations and streaks in smooth areas, they said they were "adding texture." When they smoothed the clay over rough spots, they were "adding transitions." When they added clay to weaker areas, they were "adding more supportive detail." When they moved clay from the bottom to the top or from side to side, they were "revising by moving sentences around." Sometimes they wadded up their clay and started fresh; the similarity to crumpling up a piece of paper and starting fresh was very clear.

That night, my students' assignment was to summarize what they had learned about the writing process by comparing writing an essay or story to sculpting with clay. The results demonstrated greater insight than anything I had ever gotten in response to a standard prompt, like "List and define each step in the writing process." And the quality of my students' writing that year suggested that they retained the content better, too.

Multiple Intelligences

To make your summarization assignments more compelling, you can allow students to summarize using more than one form of intelligence. According to multiple intelligences theory pioneer Howard Gardner (1993), students' proclivities are *how* they are smart, not how smart they are. Their responses are more complex and express deeper thinking and personal investment when they are allowed to make those responses in the ways in which they are smart. Considering multiple intelligences opens great avenues for summarization.

Basic Sequence

Review the basic descriptors for multiple intelligences and choose three or four intelligences that seem appropriate for the topics your students are going to summarize. Then identify one or two activities associated with those intelligences and let students choose which to take on. Here are quick descriptors for each intelligence, along with sample activities.

- *Linguistic*—This is the ability to think with words and to use language to express complex meanings. Sample activities include brainstorming, conversations, debates, public speaking, publishing, reading, rhymes, Socratic seminars, storytelling, tape-recording, tongue twisters, translations, word games, and writing.

- *Logical-Mathematical*—This is the ability to calculate, hypothesize, and quantify things. People with developed logical-mathematical intelligence can carry out complex math operations using symbolic and sequential reasoning skills, as well as inductive and deductive thinking patterns. Sample activities include brain teasers, codes, computer programming, logic puzzles, math problems, measuring, questioning, sequences, Socratic seminars, time lines, and "what if" experiments.

- *Bodily-Kinesthetic*—This is the ability to manipulate objects, including our own bodies, and to use a variety of physical skills. Individuals with strong bodily-kinesthetic intelligence have a good use of timing and mind-body coordination. Sample activities include hands-on hobbies like model building, sewing, sculpting, and woodworking, plus body metaphors, building, dance, hand gestures, jumping, movement, outdoor activities, pantomime, role-playing, sports, and touching things.

- *Spatial*—This is the ability to think in three dimensions. People with strong spatial intelligence are good at visualization, using active imagination, graphic and artistic skills, puzzles, and spatial reasoning. Sample activities involve the use of collages, colors, diagramming, drawing and doodling, jigsaw and other visual puzzles, mazes, mind maps, painting, picture metaphors, pictures and illustrations, symbols, videos, and visualizing.

- *Musical*—This is the ability to recognize, create, and reproduce music. Individuals with developed musical intelligence can figure out pitch, rhythm, timbre, and tone. They like learning with patterns, rhythm, and songs. Sample activities include attending concerts, chanting, creating jingles, doing rhythm and melody activities, humming, interpreting musical compositions, listening to music, playing instruments, singing, whistling, writing and performing rap songs, and writing lyrics.

- *Interpersonal*—This is the ability to understand and interact well with others. People with high levels of interpersonal intelligence are adept at verbal and nonverbal communication, are sensitive to the moods of others, and can accept multiple perspectives. Sample activities include being sensitive to others, board games, body sculpture with others, clubs, cooperative activities, counseling, discussion groups, group sports, leading, mediation, mentoring, partying, simulations, social activities and games, and teaching others.

- *Intrapersonal*—This is the ability to understand oneself—one's thoughts and feelings—and to use that knowledge to plan one's life. Individuals with strong interpersonal intelligence are very intuitive and reflective. Sample activities include connecting school topics to personal life, doing self-paced work at personal interest centers, planning, reading, reflecting, setting goals, spending time alone, working on individual hobbies, and writing journals.

- *Naturalist*—This is the ability to tell the differences among living things and to be sensitive to the natural world. Individuals with developed naturalist intelligence recognize patterns in society and in nature, and they like to categorize things. Sample activities include attending nature talks and videos, camping, categorizing, collecting, gardening, hiking, protecting the environment, studying plants and animals, taking care of plants and animals, telling the differences among things, using tools for investigating nature, and visiting zoos and aquariums.

- *Existentialist*—This range of abilities is not fully embraced as an intelligence, but Gardner and others have suggested it might be a ninth intelligence. People with strong existentialist intelligence are interested in the big questions of life, death, and reality: "Why are we here?" "What happens after we die?" "Is there life on other planets?" "How do we know someone is honest?" "If there is suffering in the world and I know about it, am I responsible for doing something about it?" They focus on humanity's existence. Sample activities include asking and responding to big questions, creating analogies, creating a journal, debating, dreaming, entertaining more than one possibility, looking at the root or foundation of beliefs, and reading and discussing ideologies and philosophies.

Variations and Extended Applications

For more ideas, I highly recommend Thomas Armstrong's *Multiple Intelligences in the Classroom* (2000).

An added benefit of having students who summarize using one of their developed intelligences is that it gives you a valid indicator of what they know and are able to do. For example, if you ask students to summarize only in writing, then those who don't have written language as one of their proclivities will struggle with the writing as much as with the summarizing of content. You risk diluting students' demonstration of mastery because they are struggling so much with the medium. When students summarize in a manner that is consistent with their proclivities, they are free to explore the topic and its summarization.

Maybe you can't appeal to every student's intelligence every time, but through varied and formative summarizations, you can engage most intelligences in every unit you do, especially if you offer students a choice from two or three summarization prompts or formats each time.

Another final positive feature is the emotional atmosphere of the room changes when you teach students about multiple intelligences and when you use multiple intelligences to summarize. Students see themselves as being stronger with some topics and formats and as struggling with others. They begin to accept differences in their skill levels and readiness as natural, not something to be judged as weak. They become more tolerant and encourage one another. Just because a classmate doesn't do well in one medium, doesn't mean he or she won't do especially well in another. Students also seem to be willing to try new things when struggling with academics isn't threatening. Our differences are not simply allowed; they're expected.

Letting students negotiate how they are going to summarize learning once in a while gives them ownership in the assignments. My only caution is to monitor students' choices, not because they'll take the easy way out, but because they may select too much rigor. Students get excited over alternative assignments, often designing something more complex than we teachers would have assigned. You may have to tone students down to keep their choices within reason and developmentally appropriate—more than pumping them up.

To get students to summarize using a variety of multiple intelligences, provide four or five options. Mark each activity with the associated intelligences so students can see their proclivities. Make sure to rotate all the intelligences through their multiple summarization experiences. Be aware of students who get too comfortable with the same route each time. If some students want to choose the same options every time, broaden their horizons by narrowing their choices. Allow them to choose only those that would help them grow in new directions.

As you consider your activities for multiple intelligence summarization, it's wise to make sure students can interact with the same content through each activity offered. For example, can students adequately summarize the intended video, lecture, or reading by categorizing attributes of the topic, drawing a diagram, making a journal entry, using an interpretive dance, or writing a rap song? Maybe; maybe not. Although we don't want to limit students' imaginations, we need to be reasonably sure that they encounter and express the same content no matter which route they take. With a nod to Robert Frost, it may make all the difference.

One-Word Summaries

"I have made this (letter) longer because I have not had the time to make it shorter."
—Pascal

Usually, one page of really good student writing reveals more about what the student knows than three or four pages of so-so writing does. Perhaps it's because longer pieces tempt students to stray from a clear focus; they throw in more in the hope that *something* will resonate with the teacher. Writing a small yet cogent amount about a topic is a more difficult task because every word counts; every sentence must advance the reader's understanding.

When you first tell students that you want them to create a one-word summary, they think they're getting away with something. In truth, "one word summaries" are really between a half and a full page of writing. And students soon learn that this type of summary typically requires them to invest more thought and do more work than they'd need to do for a summary three times as long.

Basic Sequence

Ask students to write one word that summarizes the lesson's topic, then to explain why they chose that word. The students' analyses require them to isolate critical attributes of the concept, person, or event, and to analyze the relevance or validity. As an alternative, ask the class collectively to brainstorm a list of word candidates, then to narrow the list to three choices from which students can choose. As the class brainstorms, students can argue for or against a word as a good one to describe the topic. No matter what they support or refute as a good description, they are analyzing the topic in a substantive manner. It's not their choice of a word that leads to learning in one-word summaries; it's their rationale.

Here are several examples of one-word summary prompts:

"The new government regulations for the meat-packing industry in the 1920s could be seen as an opportunity."

"Manufacture is not the best word to describe photosynthesis."

"Picasso's work is an argument for increasing funding for the fine arts programs in our schools."

"NASA's battles with Rockwell Industries over the warnings about frozen temperatures and the O-rings on the space shuttle were trench warfare."

Variations and Extended Applications

If you ask students to generate words for the one-word summaries, be open to connections you don't readily see. Even if students don't depict the concept or object as accurately as you'd prefer, it doesn't matter because students will see those disconnections as well, and they will attack the word's viability as a choice—interacting and summarizing while they do so. Can you see the connections between the idea of an indirect object and these one-word descriptors: beneficiary, pinball, and dependence? How about these one-word summary ideas for the concept of an adverb: catalyst, measure, steroids? Some are more accurate than others, but they all push students to examine the concepts with which they are associated.

P-M-I

Suggest this idea to your class: "Let's pay all students $25 a week for going to school. Sound OK?" Most students will agree heartily. When you do a P-M-I with them, however, at least a third will change their minds.

P-M-I stands for *pluses*, *minuses*, and *interesting*. Edward de Bono was the first to explain the technique more than two decades ago in his wonderful book, *Six Thinking Hats* (1985); the technique is still very useful today. Although some folks use P-M-I purely for getting students to consider their decisions and opinions carefully, it also makes a great summary device. After we teach students the basic procedure by making statements such as the one above or, "All students should wear only blue clothing," we can easily start using P-M-I for summarizing our lessons' content.

Basic Sequence

Ask students to set up a P-M-I chart, similar to the one in Figure 20.

— FIGURE 20 — P-M-I Chart Template		
Statement:		
Pluses	Minuses	Interesting

After students make their charts, give them a statement to consider. The statement should be about something they've been studying and should require them to use that knowledge to respond. It should present something with more than one side, and it can be worded either positively or negatively. Statements might look something like this:

"We should extend diplomatic relations with that country." (Or the opposite: "We should end diplomatic relations with that country.")

"Genetic engineering of humans should be approved by the federal government." (Or the opposite.)

"Studying grammar is the best way to learn how to write." (Or the opposite.)

"The artist's use of line and lighting are the best ways to determine a painting's quality." (Or the opposite.)

Another example might be a novel's theme, and students could state their reflections while including evidence from the novel and their own lives.

Ask students to record their response to the statement at the top of their P-M-I chart. Then have them fill in the advantages of the idea in the pluses column, the disadvantages or negatives in the minuses column, and those aspects of the idea that don't fall neatly into either category—plus or minus—in the interesting column. The students' first reflections are usually done individually.

After students finish, ask them to share their responses with a partner or small group. Announce that any ideas shared within the group can be freely "borrowed" and added to any student's recorded ideas. Encourage students who want to revise their thinking in light of what they've heard from a classmate to do so.

Variations and Extended Applications

Either you or your students can create a large version of the chart at the front of the room. Invite students or groups to help you post responses for each column, and when all the responses have been listed, ask students to reflect on where the strongest arguments lie. Usually one column has the majority of arguments, and they are often the most compelling. Students should respond purely on the evidence and not just emotion. Ask them to reexamine their initial positions. Do they still hold to what was written?

P-M-I will work well for summarization and analysis, but can also be powerful as a tool for character education experiences. These devices can teach students how to make healthy decisions regarding diet, behavior or misbehavior, exercise, drug abuse, smoking, peer pressure, and sexual behavior.

Partners A and B

Partners A and B, a technique also known as "paired verbal fluency," can be considered a type of "brain dump," similar to backing up computer work to a disk. It's a quick way to get students to process short segments of learning and to ready their brains for more learning. As mentioned in Part 1, middle and high school students learn better if they have an opportunity to interact with the content and skills they're learning about every 15 to 20 minutes. For students in elementary school, it's every 6 to 7 minutes. Teachers who chunk information in this manner help students to transfer that information to long-term memory. Partners A and B is an effective summarization tool for this kind of interaction.

Basic Sequence

Present material to students in whatever format is appropriate for your subject and grade level. After approximately 15 minutes of instruction, ask your students to choose partners (or choose for them, if that's more helpful). Identify one of them as "Partner A" and one as "Partner B." If you don't have an even number of students, make yourself the extra student's partner.

Ask Partner A in each pair to talk nonstop for one minute in a continuous flow of ideas about anything the teacher just presented or any ideas triggered by that presentation. If students get stuck, invite them to use their notes or other materials to jog their memories.

Partner B's job is to listen politely but say nothing, even if it's hard to keep quiet. (An occasional nod is OK, however.) At the end of one minute, ask Partner A to finish his or her sentence and to stop talking.

Now partner A must remain silent and listen politely as Partner B did. Partner B now talks nonstop for one minute, sharing a continuous string of ideas or thoughts related to anything in the teacher's presentation. Here's the challenge, though: Partner B may not mention anything that Partner A has already talked about.

You'll hear the Partner Bs groan and laugh a little the first time you do this, but remind them that they have their own perspectives and that their minds may go in different directions. Again, if they get stuck, they can refer to their notes and materials. Students will get better at this activity the more they do it.

When you first teach the partners A and B technique, it may take five or six minutes because of the instructions and the post-activity reflection ("What did you notice?" "What will you do to prepare for something like this in the future?"). After students are used to it, however, it will take no more than three minutes from start to finish. If one minute seems a bit long for your students at first, ask them to speak for only 30 seconds. Conversely, I've had each partner talk as long as two minutes.

Variations and Extended Applications

This technique may seem at first like an echoing activity, not a thinking activity. How can students learn from just repeating what they heard in the past 15 minutes? You'd be surprised. They must gather their thoughts about information they've just heard and then share those thoughts coherently with another student. Underlying their spoken words is the unspoken, but present, worry that they might make mistakes and be judged as incompetent by the partners. Such a concern will increase the anxiety a bit and will force them to internalize learning rather than simply respond to comprehension questions at the end of the chapter.

Two of these types of brain dumps given at separate points in a 45-minute class can be a good use of time. Don't see the summaries as a hurdle or inconvenience.

Point of View

Changing perspectives can be illuminating, no matter how small the change is. Having students manipulate information to explore an alternative viewpoint requires them to distill and review critical attributes of a topic. In this activity, the summarization doesn't come so much from the student's presentation of the point-of-view writing (or artwork or performance); it occurs in the assignment's creation. Students determine what's important as they fit things in, leave things out, and organize content coherently in the form of a compelling narrative. That's where the real learning occurs.

Basic Sequence

Ask students to retell or recount something they've learned about from a different point of view. The content could be anything: a story in their reading anthology; an account of a scientific, mathematical, or manufacturing process; a moment in history; a chemical's reaction; a concerto's performance; or the proper place for commas in a divided quote. The retelling must incorporate essential facts and concepts from the lesson.

To help students grasp the idea the first time you use this technique, call their attention to individual components of the concept, event, person, process, or object on which they need to focus. Determining individual components is easy—it's what you probably did to prepare your lessons anyway.

In a world history unit on Alexander the Great, for example, you might point out that there are many aspects of his rise to power to consider: the quarreling of the Greek city–states; Alexander's father, Philip, King of Macedonia; Persian King Darius III and the Battle of Issus in 333 BC; Syria; the use of catapults as a weapon; Persepolis; India and war elephants; and more. In a language arts unit on how to create good paragraphs, the key components might be well-chosen words, full sentences, topic sentences, supporting details, conclusions, transitions, relevancy, and more.

Once the components are listed, have your students identify a few that would offer an interesting point of view. For example, students could describe Alexander the Great from King Darius's view, from a soldier's view, or from the perspective of a catapult used by Alexander's armies. In the language arts class, they could explore paragraph construction from a transition word's point of view or from the perspective of a topic sentence trying to keep everyone rallied under one roof. Regardless of the educational discipline, students can select three or four choices and can retell what they've learned from another component's point of view. Remind them, however, that they must be accurate in every detail and as comprehensive as possible as they summarize the lessons.

Variations and Extended Applications

Here are some examples of the endless applications of point-of-view summarizations: Students might retell photosynthesis from a chloroplast's point of view or describe the performance of an intricate concerto from the cello section's perspective. They could retell the story of digestion from the points of view of the bolus passing down the esophagus, the villi in the small intestine that have capillaries receiving and carrying nutrients to the bloodstream, or a muscle in the body that finally receives the nutrients from the food ingested earlier. Students also could retell a historical incident from a biased participant's point of view. They could reveal the truth behind a pronoun being a subject or an object, according to whether it did the action or received the action.

Every alternate viewpoint invites students to consider the important features of the content in a slightly different way. By looking at different angles, they will internalize more information for a longer period of time.

P-Q-R-S-T

I learned this activity from a colleague who uses it for expository reading in his class. It's simple to remember, and it uses sound practices for reading comprehension.

Basic Sequence

To start your students with this technique, explain or show what P-Q-R-S-T stands for:

P—*Preview* to identify main parts.

Q—Develop *questions* to which you want to find answers.

R—*Read* the material, twice if possible.

S—*State* the central idea or theme.

T—*Test* yourself by answering questions (or teach the material to someone else).

The "P" and "Q" portions create an anticipation guide and prime the brain for what is to come. Although reading the material twice increases comprehension, it's not always possible in our busy world. Nonetheless, it's worth requiring once in a while. The central idea usually has two parts: the topic and the author's claim about the topic. Ask your students to find the central idea or theme for each subsection, not just a global one for the chapter. After your students have been guided through the process two or more times, assign them to do a P-Q-R-S-T process for whatever material they're studying.

The summary experience happens when students either answer their original questions or have to encapsulate the questions to teach to a classmate, parent, or teacher. For example, in the Appendix, there is a passage about censoring *Huckleberry Finn* (see sample M, p. 207). Glancing over the text, students might ask such questions as, "Why do people ban some books?" "Why is *Huckleberry Finn* so often banned?" "What did Ernest Hemingway say about *Huckleberry Finn*?" "What did Mr. Twain think about his book being banned?" Once the questions are posed, the students now have a purpose for reading: to answer those questions. By answering those questions and sharing their responses with others, students are summarizing the information. The wise teacher will direct the summarization toward the lesson's goals by inspecting and possibly revising the students' questions prior to their reading the text.

Variations and Extended Applications

If more than one student focuses on the same subsection, members of your class could critique one another's questions and responses to those questions.

This is a great instance of priming the brain. We set students up for success by helping them set a purpose for reading (to answer the questions) and by helping them structure what they are about to read. To extend this effect, ask students to pose questions in advance and present them to classmates for approval. Classmates consider the questions' relevancy and clarity. This can be done orally or in written form.

Remember, too, that when first starting with this and other summarizing techniques, choose shorter passages. A paragraph is fine. Great teachers often practice new behaviors and skills in short chunks. The task isn't so overwhelming, success is more likely, and nothing motivates like success.

Once in a while after students finish, ask them whether or not they would change their questions if they were to do it all over again, and to explain their thinking. Such analysis not only prompts students to revisit the text, but it also forces them to question their learning strategy and success—a good skill for becoming their own advocates.

RAFT

This activity teaches divergent thinking, student choice, and complexity. The acronym RAFT stands for *role, audience, form, time*.

RAFT assignments are fairly easy to put together. Figure 21 shows a RAFT list that took me about six minutes to generate. Have students consider a variety of people associated with the content (roles), a variety of people for whom or to whom the students are to communicate in those roles (audience), multiple ways in which to communicate the content (form), and a variety of settings or a specific period (time). If you don't want to add the complexity of a setting or time period, then your "T" is the topic about which students are to speak or write. Students will take on a role and will communicate a given topic to a specific audience using a specific format.

Basic Sequence

Students can choose one factor from each column and can incorporate those factors into their summarization. An example of an assignment might be a candidate for the Green Party (role) who must try to convince election board members (audience) to let her participate in a formal debate with the Democratic and Republican Party candidates. The student writes a speech (form) to give to the election board during the 2016 presidential campaign (time). To do this assignment, students will use arguments and information from past elections that had third-party candidates, as well as their knowledge of the election and debate process. Another student could be given a RAFT assignment to be a member of the election board who has just listened to the first student's speech.

After you have created lists for each column as a demonstration for your students, mix and match the lists, looking for combinations that

— FIGURE 21 — RAFT			
Role	**Audience**	**Format**	**Time (or Topic)**
Scuba diver	PTA	Deck of cards	Industrial Revolution
Ballet dancer	Kindergarteners	Travel brochure	Modern day
Comic strip character	Coast Guard	Journal entry	The Renaissance
Doctors	Parole board	Advice column	Pre–Civil War
Coach	Principal	Autobiography	Ancient Greece
Dot-com CEO	Young adolescents	Court testimony	2200
Soldier	Nursing home	Lyrics	1950
Sharecroppers	School board meeting	Field guide	1969
Mayor	Thomas Edison	Newscast	Potato famine
Mother of sick child	Zoo visitors	Fable	Late at night
Custodian	Radio listeners	Monologue	During a storm
Shoppers	Disenfranchised citizen	Posted flyers	Hot summer afternoon
Museum curator	Ancient Sumerians	Correspondence by e-mail	Cuban Missile Crisis
Judge	Journalists	Political cartoon	At Hogwarts School

suggest interesting and substantive interactions. If you as the teacher see any elements in any column that seem frivolous, consider removing them from the choices. There's no sense in setting your students up with something of dubious value. Of course, students can create their own columns after doing a few of these with you.

Note that the ideas in Figure 21's RAFT list example apply to general subjects, not a specific subject, and the selections of people, audiences, and formats are random. If you are doing a specific unit, purposefully align the choices with subject-related people, audiences, and formats.

Variations and Extended Applications

Students get to choose how they express content, and this personal choice and opportunity to express creativity helps to generate ownership of the task. On RAFT activities, motivation is usually pretty high. Be open to combinations that you don't see at first. As long as students demonstrate a good grasp of what's being summarized, unconventional approaches aren't a bad thing. In fact, for the kind of students we teachers want in our classrooms and eventually leading society, it's probably a good thing.

Save the Last Word for Me

Here is another technique that appeals to the brain's innately social nature. It's nominally focused on group discussion of text-based learning, but it's actually reliant on a prereading process during which each student identifies a phrase from the text that he or she will be the last one to comment on during the discussion to follow.

Basic Sequence

Ask your students to read the assigned passage either the night before or in class before the discussion. If possible, ask them to make reading notations in light pencil to support their ideas (see the suggestions of reading notations in Part 2). After students have read the material, ask them to identify three or more sentences they'd like to discuss. Those sentences might anger them, pose a conflict, confuse them, or support or challenge something they believe. Remind them that they will choose only one of the three sentences to offer the group, but they need to have alternate choices in case their first and second choices are taken by someone else.

Once they have read and identified the talking point sentences, divide your students into groups of four to five. Ask one member of each group to read a line that he or she has marked. Even if the line wasn't marked with standard reading notations, it should be one identified as worth discussing. This first person will read a sentence aloud but won't add any comments or any response. In turn, each of the remaining group members will react by agreeing, refuting, supporting, clarifying, commenting, or questioning. After everyone has had a chance to respond, the originator of the line gets to offer a commentary, thus getting the last word on the topic.

When this round of discussion is done, the next person in the circle reads a sentence, and everyone responds. So it goes with each member of the group. This process can take anywhere from 15 to 45 minutes to complete, depending on the size of your groups and how experienced your students are.

Variations and Extended Applications

When I've done this technique with students, they've really gotten into it like scholars. The best part is that by the time the group finishes, they have encountered most of the salient points from the reading selection. All I have to do is facilitate a classwide discussion in which we debrief what each group has discussed.

It's fun to watch statement originators trying to keep calm while waiting their turn to have the last word. They see what decorum can be worth, however. They can't complain that they can't get a word in edgewise or that they can never get the last word. For many students, this technique is more than just an effective way to summarize; it's a step forward in maturation.

Share One; Get One

Share One; Get One is another quick processing technique that works as a "brain dump" to break lectures and other extended learning experiences into smaller chunks. These miniprocessing activities can be done anywhere, any time, as long as students have paper and pencil or pen.

Basic Sequence

Present the lesson's concepts and skills as you normally would. When it's time to take a break and have students process what has been presented, ask them to draw a grid of nine squares, big enough to cover at least half a sheet of notebook paper (see Figure 22).

In any three squares of the matrix, ask students to record three different concepts, facts, or skills they recall from the presentation. Now ask your students to get up from their seats and move around the room asking classmates to fill in the remaining squares with concepts, facts, and skills that haven't yet been recorded on the matrix. Each classmate can add only one idea to another classmate's matrix, but students can add ideas to as many classmates' matrices as they wish. The task is complete when six different classmates have filled all remaining six squares with different concepts, facts, or skills. Then students may return to their seats.

Variations and Extended Applications

At this point, you can decide to simply restate what students have done so far. However, it's even more effective to ask students to write a coherent summary of the presentation using information recorded in their matrices. Have your students put the concepts, facts, and skills in logical order and to rewrite the points from each square in sentence form. This manipulation of content and skills into a particular format is very effective because it forces students to interact with the material, not just record it. This step can be an in-class or at-home assignment.

If you're looking for a quick way for students to process what is presented while relieving the stress on bone growth plates that is caused by sitting and that distracts so many young adolescent and adolescent students from their learning, Share One; Get One is a welcome strategy to use.

— FIGURE 22 —
Share One; Get One: Story Analysis

Exposition: – Setting, mood – main characters – major conflict introduced ...	**Rising Action:** – The major and minor conflicts of the story – Moving toward the climax ...	**✳ CLIMAX ✳** The most exciting part of the story
Resolution: The natural ending — when major conflicts are resolved/dealt with in some way.	Four types of conflict • Character vs. nature • Character vs. society • two different forces within one character • character/group vs. character/group	Plot: The events that move the story along
Touching Spirit Bear (Mikaelson) • character vs. nature (boy alone on island) • character vs. society (circle justice response from community) • two different forces within one character (boy confronting his own anger)	Stories have a beginning, middle, and end	"Somebody-Wanted-But-So" is a good way to summarize plot

Socratic Seminars

Socrates knew how to get students and citizens to confront their basic assumptions and to learn from the analysis. His technique of questioning and ongoing discussion is still one of the best ways to illuminate content. Students can participate in such experiences before a unit to help prime their minds for what is to come, but they get even more out of the experience when they have studied the concepts to be discussed. In a Socratic seminar, students process, apply, and extend what they've been learning. It's summarization, but it's also good instruction. And hemlock cocktails are not involved. Let's take a look at a Socratic approach in action:

"Should some books be banned in public schools?" the teacher asked.

"Yes," said Ryan, a student in the second row. "If the book goes against the community's values."

The teacher arched an eyebrow. "That's a more conservative view than others of your age have espoused, Ryan."

Ryan shrugged in response. The teacher continued. "And how are a community's values determined?"

"By what the majority wants," Ryan replied.

"So minority opinions should not count?"

"No, they count, just not as much."

"How much do they count?" the teacher asked. "Whose values win? If I'm a parent and I want the school library to remove a book because I find it offensive, should my one vote count enough to have it removed from the shelves?"

"No," Ryan replied again.

"What if there are 10 of us who object to the book?"

"We have to be reasonable," Ryan said. "Whatever the majority wants, that's the community's value, and that's how school librarians should respond. They have a responsibility to protect kids from scary and sexual things. I mean, I don't want my 5th grade sister reading Stephen King novels."

"Where's the cutoff line? At what age do some novels become OK while others are still prohibited? Does it change for different novels? For different individuals?"

"Maybe," Ryan said.

The teacher paused before the next question. "There was a time in our country when the majority of folks in certain communities were racist and mistreated those of different cultures or skin colors. Should these kinds of community majority values be protected?"

"No, of course not," Ryan said. "The federal government must step in and do something when people are being abused because of their skin color."

"So when it comes to books, the majority of the community rules, but when it comes to human rights abuses, we turn it over to the federal government to decide for us?"

"I guess so," Ryan replied.

The teacher nodded. "That's been done both very successfully and very poorly during our country's history. It's often a point of contention between political parties. Let's examine this idea: What are the criteria under which it is appropriate for the federal government to get involved with a small community's values? And is federal government policymaking at the local level a good or bad thing for the country as a whole?"

Where does the summarization occur? During the preparation and reflection before the seminar, during the seminar discussion itself, and during postseminar reflection and evaluation. This kind of active learning requires students to consider the concepts and facts as they respond to questions and as they hear their classmates' responses. The information and understandings will stay with students beyond next week's quiz.

Basic Sequence

Before discussing as part of a Socratic seminar, students need information and a common frame of reference, which will come in many forms: discussions, field trips, labs, lectures, readings, research, simulations, videos, and more. These preseminar experiences should be rich with ideas and "discussability," that is, more than one point of view, potentially contradicting ideas, and relevance to other learning and real-life situations. Besides the experiences themselves, students should have time to reflect on the learning before the seminar. They might prepare by answering guided questions, creating graphic organizers, doing artwork, having small group discussions, using journals or learning logs, and applying other techniques.

Most Socratic seminars are conducted with students sitting in a circle, their notes and other materials in their laps and available for reference. With 32 students or more in a class, however, some classrooms cannot accommodate such a large circle. In addition, larger circles don't allow all students to participate as much as smaller circles do. To maximize participation, conduct two Socratic seminar circles, each with only half the class. Conduct one seminar while the rest of the class observes and provides feedback using a set of agreed-to criteria for seminar success. During the second half of class or on the second day, have the groups switch so that those who were observing and providing feedback are now conducting the seminar, and those who were in the seminar are now observing and providing feedback. Sometimes I've had two seminars going at the same time, which can be both noisy and confusing.

For us teachers, the hardest part of Socratic seminars is staying quiet and letting students do the talking. Do whatever it takes to keep from jumping in: tape your mouth shut, sit on your hands, look at your shoes, but make sure students are the ones doing most of the talking. You do need to give students the tools to keep conversations going, however: (1) Teach them how to develop good discussion questions that aren't just for "yes" or "no" answers, (2) teach them how and when to ask follow-up questions, and (3) give them a list of questions to choose from as they keep the conversation going. They will eventually outgrow the lists as their proficiency increases.

To begin a seminar, throw the first question to the group, and make it provocative.

Teacher: Students, today's Socratic seminar is about censorship. You've all read and reflected on the topic in a number of ways. Now we're ready to apply and review what you've learned. Please open your seminar discussion with a response to one of the following quotes from Nat Hentoff's *The Day They Came to Arrest the Book.*

- "Adults are free to read anything they like—because they are responsible for themselves—young people are not—and cannot be—wholly responsible for themselves. And so . . . the school, by law, has the responsibility for determining what students shall read."
- "Freedom is a dangerous word."
- "It is only in the free marketplace of ideas that truth will prevail."
- "The best way to deal with vicious lies, my friend, is to not give them a chance to infect people. Giving those so-called ideas the respectability of a debate helps them spread."

Jared: I'll begin. Debating ideas doesn't give hurtful ideas more respect. It's better if we get bad ideas out where everyone can see how bad they are. Look at what happened with children during the industrial revolution.

And off we go. The best openings don't always have to use quotations. They can be simple starters: "Why is this called _____?" "What is _____ about?" "Why would someone want to _____?" "How is _____ really about _____?"

As students talk with one another, they must be careful to back up their claims with evidence. Encourage them to provide supportive details and evidence from the notes they have on hand as well as their observations, readings, and reflections. If students don't back up their claims with evidence, invite other classmates to question them about it: They can ask questions such as "Can you back that up?" "How does that relate to what we're talking about?" "Help me understand your reasoning."

A good general tip for managing interaction is to ask students to refer to classmates by name when they want to add to the discussion. It helps keep decorum: "I disagree with Charlotte." "If you add that to what Lamont was saying. . . ." "Jenny has it right. . . ."

The teacher's role in the seminar is (1) to keep the discussion going by throwing out another provocative question, (2) to make sure nothing inaccurate is communicated by asking clarifying questions when misconceptions are stated, and (3) to get out of the way and let the students talk. You can also take notes for evaluation and can make sure appropriate citizenship and group processes are maintained.

Sometimes we get students who have difficulty participating in Socratic seminars. If you have chronic interrupters, challenge them to speak only after every fourth person has spoken, and point out that because they will get perhaps two more contributions before the end of the discussion, they should choose their comments wisely.

Then there is the flip side: students who don't contribute enough. They might be shy, intimidated, or otherwise uncomfortable with the experience. Although you should affirm the other students' efforts to invite quiet classmates to participate, also stress the need to respect quiet students' reticence. Tell the class to remember that just because someone is not speaking up doesn't mean they are not listening or are unprepared. If it works better for quieter students, let them summarize orally five major points discussed. Thus, they report what others have said and not what they believe themselves. You're still asking them to speak publicly, but it's not as threatening.

Good Socratic seminars have good closings. Invite a few students to come up with closing questions or offer some yourself: "What would _____ think of our arguments today?" "Did we answer the question?" "How does this relate to _____?"

After the seminar has concluded, make sure students receive feedback from the observers and from you. Encourage their own reflections on how they did. To provide feedback, consider videotaping 20 minutes of the Socratic seminar and playing it back for students. Seeing themselves is a powerful tool for learning.

Variations and Extended Applications

In Socratic seminars, it's important to have the "big picture" in your teacher mind, but to also be open to new directions posed by the students during the course of the conversation. We don't want to limit them to our thinking or guide them to our "correct" interpretations. Even though most of the talking is done by students, teachers can change the emphasis and results of Socratic seminars by the questions they pose or deny. Let the seminars live up to Socrates' legacy, however: the questioning of assumptions, the free exploration of ideas.

Also, it's wise to make students aware of the nature of free-flowing group discussions. In some situations, a subset or whole group of participants can "gang up" on a student with an alternative viewpoint, making the student feel insecure or hurt. Stress that as long as someone has a well-considered rationale for his or her point of view, that idea is worthy of examination.

Finally, although it's most commonly associated with Mortimer Adler's Padeia Schools, the Socratic seminar has taken on a life of its own in schools and conferences around the world. Adapt it for your own students' needs. If you have to change the rules slightly in order to enhance the experience or effectiveness or to be sensitive to a student, do it.

Something-Happened-and-Then/Somebody-Wanted-But-So

As I teacher, I know that I don't always have time to spend mulling over what the best graphic organizer or summarization technique might be for every single text students must read. Sometimes, I just want a fill-in-the-blank template and a quick, one-or-two-sentence format that will help my students summarize. This technique succeeds on both counts, and it's suitable for both nonfiction texts (as Something-Happened-and-Then) and fiction texts (as Somebody-Wanted-But-So). I learned it from my department chair and a learning disabilities specialist, and I can attest that it helps promote the success of even the most academically challenged students.

Basic Sequence

Provide the following set of prompts (a template) to students before they read nonfiction or experience the learning:

> Something (independent variable) . . .
> Happened (change in that independent variable) . . .
> And (effect on the dependent variable) . . .
> Then (conclusion).

The goal is to use the template to write a one- or two-sentence summary of a longer piece. A good example of this technique in action is to share an article on water erosion and to have the students complete the template. A student might read the lengthy article and boil it down to this "Heavy rains washed away the soil, making it nearly impossible for plants to grow there." It is short and to the point, and it has a general overview that includes the topic, a significant point about the topic, and the conclusion.

146

Students can do the same thing with fiction but with a different template:

>Somebody (characters) . . .
>
>Wanted (plot motivation) . . .
>
>But (conflict) . . .
>
>So (resolution).

A good practice for this technique is to summarize a favorite passage, theme, or characteristic from a popular novel or television show.

>In *Harry Potter and the Sorcerer's Stone*, Hermione *wanted* to be accepted as a respected student at Hogwarts School for Witchcraft and Wizardry, *but* those who resented her muggle ancestry constantly thwarted her efforts, *so* she worked twice as hard to be better than everyone else in her studies.

Notice how easy it is to apply this fiction technique to nonfiction summaries of anything that can be told in narrative form:

>FDR wanted to restore U.S. prosperity during his presidency, *but* the long years of the Depression had suppressed the economy and citizens' morale to the point at which current government practices couldn't bring them back. *So* he redefined the government's role in economic stimulation with his radical "New Deal."

Variations and Extended Applications

If you want a more elaborate summarization, you could ask students to use the sentences they create from the template as a topic sentence and provide three supportive details.

This technique is "a foot in the door"' for many students who find summarizing difficult. Even students two or more years below grade level usually find success with these basic templates. For some, however, you may have to write it out with blank lines in which students insert the material like a closure activity, while others can grab the words and structure their response on their own.

The first time you use these templates with students, it may be helpful to provide the information that needs to go in the blanks in a separate list—leaving it to students to connect the prompts to the correct responses. Once students have matched prompts and responses, ask them to write the one- or two-lined summarization with everything flowing and intact. Also, stop for a moment, and ask students how these different segments best flow. This might include discussions of transition words, punctuation, and staying focused on the definitions of the terms (i.e., "somebody" refers to the main character, "wanted" refers to the major plot motivation in the story, and so on). By the way, if students create summarizations using these templates that deviate from what you intended, ask students to give their reasoning for their choices. Their interpretations may work just as well.

Sorting Cards

This technique appeals to tactile and kinesthetic students and to those who like fitting together puzzles and deciphering mystery clues. It's well worth the bit of preparation required.

Basic Sequence

After you've taught your students something that has multiple categories, such as cycles in science, multiple ideologies, multiple theorems in geometry, systems of the body, taxonomic nomenclature, or types of government, they're ready to do a sorting cards summarization. On a bulletin board, chalkboard, or poster board, place the titles of the categories being studied. Then provide students with index cards or sticky notes on which you have recorded the individual facts, concepts, and attributes of the categories. Allow the students to work in groups so they place each fact, concept, or attribute in its correct category.

Summarization occurs every time a card is lifted, as students weigh decisions about where it belongs. The conversation among group members is almost as important to the learning experience as the placement of the cards, so let students defend their reasoning orally and often. If one student questions another's placement, the discussion will further the effect. Any dissent will result in students referencing their notes and textbooks for more information, and it's teaching nirvana.

Variations and Extended Applications

If it's hard to set this up vertically, don't be afraid to push back the desks and tables and to do the activity on the floor, in the hallway, or in another room entirely.

To have students do this individually, ask them to cut out little pieces of paper (one for each fact, concept, or attribute) in advance so they can record the terms on each piece. If they place everything in an envelope or plastic bag, then they can practice the activity at home. The next day in class, group the students and have them defend their categorization. For an added challenge, after students have categorized the ideas successfully, ask them to sort the items another way, according to different criteria.

Spelling Bee de Strange

If you want to review spellings and definitions in a fun way, this technique works well. Instead of a normal spelling bee, try the "de Strange" version, in which students substitute agreed-upon sound effects (usually animal or nonsense noises) for all vowels.

"Palindrome is spelled, P – achoo – L – ribbit-ribbit – N – D – R – oo-la-la – M – [thblphht!]" said Anna proudly.

"Mr. Smith," Stevie called out, "she should have hee-haw'd instead of ribbit-ribbiting after the L."

Mr. Smith considered the spelling of the word before responding. "No, Stevie, she has it right. Hee-haw is not in the word. That's ribbit-ribbit. Now, a question to the other team: For five points, can you define the term?"

As one team tries to spell the words while keeping a straight face, the other team makes sure the words are correctly spelled using the correct letters and sounds in the correct sequences.

Basic Sequence

Create two teams just as you would in a regular spelling bee, and have them alternate spelling words aloud. Rotate all team members through the spelling hot seat. Remember, students may not use any vowels, only the corresponding sounds that the students assign. To keep students on their toes, give points to the listening team if they find mistakes in the presenting team's spelling, and take points off if their assertion is wrong.

Invite students to make up their own noises for each vowel (or possibly each phoneme). If you prefer a starting point, here are a few that have been very successful:

A = "achoo"
E = "thblphht!" (Bronx cheer)
I = "ribbit-ribbit"
O = "oo-la-la!" (or "oink-oink")
U = "hee-haw" (or "sooooowee!" or "burble")

Variations and Extended Applications

To add fun and complexity, consider increasing the speed. The faster the presenting team can spell each word, the more outrageous the sound of the word and the more difficult it is for the listening team to detect an error. You can also increase the variety of sounds and elements students have to consider if you assign different phonemes different sounds. For example, a long "e" sound (as in "meek") might have the corresponding noise "eekeek." The schwa "e" sound (as in "ensemble") might have the corresponding noise "uh-oh," and the short "e" sound (as in "bet") might have the Bronx cheer or "raspberry" noise "thblphht!" (Ripple the cheeks and lips as you execute this one.) Students should account for all those vowel noises, not just simple one-to-one letter-noise correlations.

There will be a lot of laughter, as well as some serious competition and a review of vocabulary terms. People walking by your classroom may stop and peer into your room, wondering what planet your students are from, which adds to the enjoyment. Nod a smiling "hello," ask your students to recite their vowels (noise correlations only), and continue with the Spelling Bee de Strange as if nothing were amiss. It isn't.

SQ3R

Many of us grew up with this classic summarization technique. It still works today and is used most often for textbook chapters or for research or news articles. SQ3R stands for *survey, question, read, recite,* and *review.* SQ3R's structure appeals to many students, so it's worth adding to your repertoire of approaches.

Basic Sequence

In the first step, *survey,* students read the headings of each section of a textbook chapter, as well as the first sentence of each paragraph. They also look at the graphics, and they read the chapter summary to get an overview. When the survey is over, students turn the headings into *questions* to set a purpose for reading. For example, the section title "Freedmen's Bureau Brings Change" becomes the question "What was the Freedmen's Bureau and how did it affect the South?" The questions can then be written down as prompts for note-taking.

After students have surveyed the text and formed their questions, they are ready for the first of the three Rs: *read.* They read the text to answer their questions, and they write down the information in note form under each question. In the second R, *recite,* students cover their answers to the questions and read just the questions, reciting the answers from memory. Of course, they may lift their hands to check the accuracy and comprehensiveness of their responses. It's often helpful to do this step as a T-chart or T-list (see page 164).

The final R is for *review.* Students write a summary of what they've learned using the answers to their questions. If the answer to any question is a little thin, students will go back to reread the text material and then fill in the missing pieces. The review can be done in other formats too: artistically, musically, orally, and physically.

Variations and Extended Applications

Like many other summarization techniques, SQ3R benefits from specific modeling. Think-alouds are a great way to do this. Begin by giving everyone a copy of the original text, but have an enlarged, markable version for yourself that all students can see ("Smartboards," projected overhead transparencies, computers with television monitors suspended from the ceiling, or newsprint work well).

As you do each step of SQ3R, share your thoughts, no matter how insignificant. These should be thoughts on procedure, content, structures, and personal reactions to the content. It's a bit like an oral stream of consciousness, but pause periodically and ask students what you're going to think next: "Okay, I have to do this 'recite' part of SQ3R. How shall I set it up?"

Pause here and ask students what they recommend. "The best way for me right now is to write the answers on the left side of a vertically folded piece of paper, then write the answers on the right side of the fold. To do the reciting, I'll crease the paper along the fold and flip back and forth, testing myself. But what if I have something wrong on my paper? How will I know I'm learning the right answers?" Pause once again and ask students for suggested responses.

Remember that think-alouds are more effective teaching tools if students do them in front of each other. Ask a student who's willing to act a bit to do a demonstration of SQ3R in front of the class. In advance, however, prepare the student so that he applies several great SQ3R moves and several moves that violate proper SQ3R protocols. When the student does his think-aloud, tell the rest of the class that they are looking for proper and improper techniques according to the SQ3R process. Afterward, let the class critique the student's demonstration.

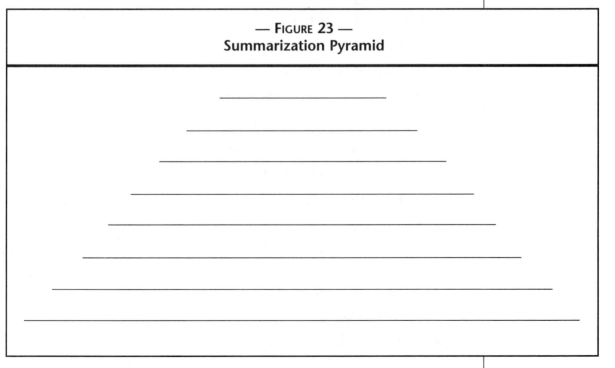

Summarization Pyramids

Summarization pyramids are wonderfully versatile. They come in many formats, have many possible sizes, and use many different prompts. It's a cinch to adapt the basic foundation of this technique to your curriculum and your students' needs.

Basic Sequence

Construct a pyramid of lines on a sheet of paper. When first playing with this format, begin with eight lines, as shown in Figure 23.

— FIGURE 23 —
Summarization Pyramid

For each line, choose prompts that yield one-word or short answers for the shorter lines, longer responses for longer lines. If you have a large pyramid and a prompt that requires a lengthy response, consider asking students to use more than one line of the pyramid for their response. Suggested prompts include the following:

- A synonym for the topic

- An analogy between the topic and a sport

- One question it sparks in you

- Three attributes or facts about the topic

- Three words that best describe the topic

- A book title or news headline that would capture the essence of the topic

- One or two other topics related to this topic

- Causes of the topic

- Effects of the topic

- Reasons we study the topic

- Arguments for the topic

- Ingredients of the topic

- Personal opinion on the topic

- Demonstration of the topic in action

- The larger category from which this topic comes

- A formula or sequence associated with the topic

- Insight gained from studying the topic

- Tools for using the topic

- Three moments in the history of the topic

- One thing we used to think about the topic that we've discovered to be incorrect

- Samples of the topic

- People who use the topic

- What the topic will be like in 25 years

This list could go on forever. As you decide on prompts and pyramid sizes, make sure to choose experiences that will allow students to interact with the intended topic in many ways. To learn something from more than one angle is to learn that something well. Five to eight lines is generally a good summarization length, but don't be afraid to go longer with some topics.

Variations and Extended Applications

Are there other shapes that lend themselves to these types of prompts? Sure. Ask students to respond to similar prompts as they create a learning tree with many branches. Roots could elicit responses that refer to the causes of things, while the branches could refer to the products (fruits) of those elements listed in the roots.

The shape of the structure could have something to do with the topic, too: a ziggurat to express information about Mesopotamia and the Fertile Crescent, clouds with various forms of precipitation to express information about the water cycle or types of clouds, a Yucca plant (leaves pointing up) to express information about the desert, a bar graph or pie chart to express information about graphing data.

Summary Ball

Yes, this technique incorporates actual projectiles. If your classroom contains a lot of student projects, a lot of decorations hanging from the ceiling, or a lot of aquariums or terrariums, you may want to skip this one. If your room is relatively clear of these potential, yet unintended, targets, then give this technique a try. I've never had a class that didn't enjoy it.

Basic Sequence

Present your material as you normally would: artwork, demonstration, discussion, field trip, lecture, reading, video, writing, or worksheets. After a critical mass of information has been presented, ask students to stand at their desks. If their placement in the class is too cumbersome for gently tossing objects to one another, ask students to form a larger—though probably wobbly—circle around the desks or tables.

Begin the activity by tossing an inflated beach ball to any student. The student who catches the ball has three seconds to state any fact, concept, or skill recently presented in the lessons. He then tosses the ball to another student in the room who has not yet spoken. The second student states a fact, concept, or skill that hasn't been mentioned, then tosses the ball to another student, and so on. If a student can't think of something from the lesson, he still tosses the ball, but then must sit down and is out of play. The game continues until only one student is left standing.

In my classes, we often get down to two or three students, and no one can think of anything else from the lesson, so we call it a tie. The game can be very exciting if it gets down to two people and they have remembered enough from the lesson to do a dramatic back-and-forth with the ball while zinging facts, concepts, and skills at each other.

Variations and Extended Applications

If a beach ball gets a little stale or worn over the year, consider another object—one that is soft but tossable. In the past, I've used a foam rubber fish (we play "Summary Fish"), a Nerf ball, a tennis ball, and those bags of fake eyeballs in thick, viscous liquid that you find in magic shops and toy stores. (Yes, I was teaching middle school at the time.) The kids enjoyed all of them.

Students have only three seconds to respond, so this game goes fast. In a class of 32 students, for example, if every student remembers one fact, concept, or skill and communicates it successfully, one full round of ball tossing takes about five minutes. It's rare that the students think of 32 different items, however, so you might modify the activity.

First, consider increasing participation for all students by forming two, three, or four groups, each with its own ball or object to toss so everyone gets to offer two or three items before having to sit down. Second, consider allowing any item to be repeated once (to a total of two times) instead of being stated only once. Repetition reinforces information in students' minds and makes it easier for those students who are struggling to stay in the game.

Once again, this summarization strategy enables students to review material while physically moving. It relieves the stresses on the bone growth plates and the muscle movement gets oxygen and nutrients to the brain—something rather vital to cognition.

Synectic Summaries

I first encountered synectics as a teaching tool when I read the work of William J. J. Gordon (1961) back in the 1970s. He defined synectics as "the joining together of different and apparently irrelevant elements" or, put more simply, "making the familiar strange." The premise for using synectics as a summarizing technique is to have students look at the critical attributes of something under study in unusual ways and, through this unconventional analysis, come away with a deeper understanding of it than they would have gotten from a quick "define the terms" type of assignment.

Synectics requires an atmosphere that promotes creativity and positive risk-taking, so if your students are prone to put-downs or hurtful judgments of others, it may not be the best technique. But if the environment is right the results can be tremendous, with students experiencing mini-epiphanies when they draw illuminating analogies between school topics and something found in everyday life. Learning transcends classroom walls.

Basic Sequence

After students have had some experience with a topic, ask them to describe the topic, focusing on descriptive words and critical attributes. This activity is more successful when done in small groups, but it can be done individually. The activity may take a few minutes in class or it can be an overnight homework assignment.

When you first introduce synectics as a summary technique, give an example, such as the following:

Topic: Romeo and Juliet

Brainstormed description: tragedy, parents, Montagues, Capulets, family feud, Verona, marriage, masked ball, Friar Lawrence, Nurse, Tybalt, Mercutio, friendship, homicide, sword fighting, Paris, banishment, tomb, messenger, suicide, poison, sorrow, Shakespeare

The next step is to identify an unrelated category to compare to the descriptions above. You can tailor the category to the developmental level of your students. For example, for younger students, you can compare *Romeo and Juliet* to other stories or movies before you start comparing it to physical objects. With older students, however, you could ask them to compare *Romeo and Juliet* to items found in a kitchen: a blender, a kitchen timer, a sink disposal, a drying rack for dishes.

Here's one to use when teaching students about the endocrine system: "Think of a sport that reminds you of the endocrine system. Explain why you chose that sport by writing or expressing the analogy between the two."

A student might write: "The endocrine system is like playing zones in basketball. Each player, or gland, is responsible for his area of the game." As your students continue to flesh out their analogies, they'll develop mental dexterity with the information about the endocrine system. They're learning more than they would by reading a textbook chapter and answering the comprehension questions on a specific page.

Variations and Extended Applications

Once students get the idea, give them a category that requires more mental dexterity; they'll learn more. If the category is too similar to the concept you're teaching, students' analysis is more a matter of drawing lines from aspects of one process to similar aspects of another, thus becoming more of a matching activity than a thinking activity. The more students think about and discuss their descriptions with classmates, the more they summarize and internalize the information, while satisfying the socially interactive nature of the mind.

One way to increase the challenge is to ask students to do 4-Square Synectics. In this type of summarizing, the class brainstorms four objects from a particular general category you've given them, such as a circus, a coral reef, a favorite book, a favorite sport, household items, kitchen appliances, musical instruments, rock or rap music concerts, and shopping malls. Once the category is identified, list on the chalkboard or overhead the first four items your students mentioned as being commonly found in the chosen context. Then ask your students to work in small groups and to determine the connections or similarities between the lesson learning and the listed objects.

Figure 24 shows an empty synectic summary matrix for the question "How was the Marshall Plan, which was endorsed by President Harry Truman, like each of these four musical instruments?"

— FIGURE 24 — Synectic Summary Matrix: The Marshall Plan
How Was the Marshall Plan Like Each of These Musical Instruments?

saxophone	drum set
trumpet	guitar

Students might claim the Marshall Plan was like a *trumpet* whose high, bright notes were the calls to all European nations to rally around the cause of rebuilding Europe into a prosperous continent. The *drums* kept the rhythm of the labor forces' steady march onward, building house after house, repairing electrical systems, and repaving roads. *Guitars* can be strummed, all the strings at once, or plucked, string by string. The students might say this shows that sometimes the countries worked together, while at other times, as with the Soviet countries, they wanted to rebuild alone, without U.S. aid. And everyone was always careful not to wind the strings too tightly for fear one of them would snap. Some nations were suspicious of the President Truman's seemingly unselfish offers of aid, so the president had to step carefully. The *saxophone's* mournful-yet-ready-to-turn-upbeat voice, the students might say, reminds us of our common humanity and the somber impact of WWII on the world, and how important it was to the whole world that the U.S. be generous to both allies and former enemies instead of vengeful. Just as music from the saxophone helps men see each other as brothers, an important aspect of the Marshall Plan was for the U.S. not to do the rebuilding itself, but to aid countries in their own efforts, working side by side, sharing the wisdom necessary to get the job done.

When your students finish all four analogies, ask members of each group to share their analogies aloud. Then invite the rest of the class to constructively critique the analogies in terms of accuracy and applicability. The first point of learning is the genesis of the analogies. The second, and sometimes more effective point, is the group's critique of a classmate's analogy. Try to leave time for such valuable discussion.

One last reminder: Students are very creative and often see connections and similarities that teachers might not see. Once again, we must not limit our students to our own imagination. Like many adults, we give our internal editors too much power and are not willing to open our minds to initially bizarre connections for fear that they'll lead us nowhere or that the ideas will be rejected by others. Let's not impose that thinking on the next generation.

T-Chart/T-List

Many students are not able to read or experience content on their own or to determine what is salient from the experience until their late high school years—if then. Throughout most of the formal schooling years, students need mindful teachers to structure content and skills in a manner that will help them to retrieve and retain information for the long term. Using a T-chart, or T-list as it is sometimes called, primes the brain for learning and structures information for storage. T-charts also make great study guides.

Basic Sequence

Before students read text material, watch a video or a demonstration, go on a field trip, or listen to a lecture, give them a partially completed T-chart. Figure 25 shows an example of a T-chart used for analyzing President Woodrow Wilson's 14-point speech of 1918.

The left side of the chart can show general concepts or questions while the right usually can show more details. We can provide students with the main ideas or questions and have them determine the supporting details or evidence. Or we might provide the supporting detail or evidence and have them determine the main ideas or questions. We could even provide a mixture of the two and have students fill in the empty portions. The idea is to establish a purpose and a structure for learning. Asking students to design their own T-charts after the class has previewed the textbook chapter or learning experience is also effective. Before doing this, however, provide several opportunities for students to use T-charts you've already created. They need to see the T-chart's value before creating ones of their own.

— FIGURE 25 — T-Chart: Wilson Peace Plan	
Main Ideas	**Details or Examples**
Three reasons President Wilson designed the plan for peace	1. 2. 3.
Three immediate effects on U.S. allies	1. 2. 3.
Three protocols created by the plan	1. 2. 3.

When students have completed their T-charts, they've also created a practical study guide. Ask them to fold their T-charts along the vertical centerline. Now they can test themselves by flipping back and forth between main ideas or questions and the supporting details or answers.

Anything in our curriculum that lends itself to separation and study like this can be expressed in a T-chart, such as the following:

- Main ideas and their supporting details
- Questions and answers
- Claims and arguments for the claims
- Categories and examples
- Antonyms
- Causes and effects
- Problems and solutions
- Terms and their definitions
- Analogies and real-life examples
- Before and after

• Things associated with one category, person, concept, place, or time, plus things associated with another category, person, concept, place, or time

Variations and Extended Applications

Readers who are familiar with the Cornell Note-Taking System shown in Figure 26 will recognize T-charts as two-thirds of the basic format for that system. All you need to add to create the Cornell approach is to draw a horizontal line across the bottom of the chart and to ask students to write in the space below that line a three- to five-sentence summary of the information given in the chart. With its consistent success record, the Cornell Note-Taking System is worth considering:

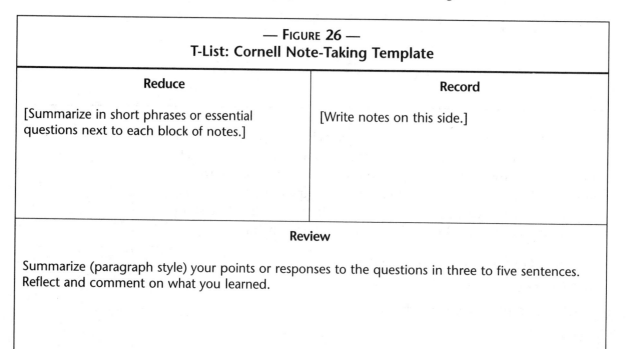

— FIGURE 26 —
T-List: Cornell Note-Taking Template

Reduce	**Record**
[Summarize in short phrases or essential questions next to each block of notes.]	[Write notes on this side.]

Review

Summarize (paragraph style) your points or responses to the questions in three to five sentences. Reflect and comment on what you learned.

T-charts are easy to teach and use, and they are among the techniques students will remember and use in later years. They work well with students of all performance levels, including those with learning disabilities.

Taboo®

Quick: Get someone to guess the phrase "latitude and longitude" without pointing to anything in the room, without gesturing, and without using any of the following words in your clues: coordinates, degree, Greenwich, grid, international, lines, map, meridians, parallels, prime, or any number. These words are forbidden, or "taboo."

The technique, familiar from the popular Milton Bradley board game, is difficult at first, but students soon become comfortable circumnavigating the taboo words and find innovative ways to describe the word's definition.

Where does the summarization occur? Two places: first, when students create their own decks of Taboo cards, and second, when they try to guess what the speaker is trying to get them to say during the game itself.

Taboo is also great for assessing information. When students create a Taboo card for a word, they list what they consider to be salient associations. By just glancing at the cards, you can assess what the students took away from the learning experience.

Basic Sequence

To prepare the students, play a demonstration game as a whole class, using a set of about 30 Taboo cards related to previous topics of study.

To make a Taboo card, turn an index card vertically and write a concept or vocabulary word at the top. Place a thick line underneath that word. In the remaining space under the line, write five to seven words or concepts your students would normally associate with the word above the line. Figure 27 shows three examples.

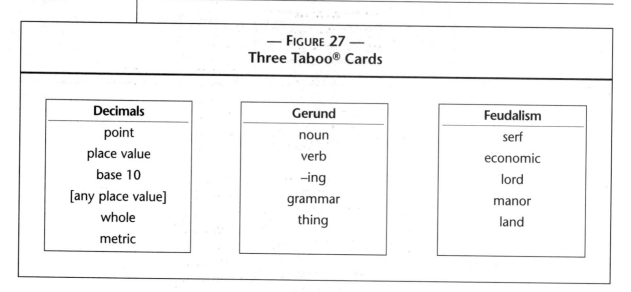

— FIGURE 27 —
Three Taboo® Cards

Decimals	Gerund	Feudalism
point	noun	serf
place value	verb	economic
base 10	–ing	lord
[any place value]	grammar	manor
whole	thing	land
metric		

To play a game of Taboo, you'll need a deck of prepared Taboo cards, a timer (a watch is fine), and a buzzer (or a squeaky toy that becomes a "poor man's buzzer").

Divide the class into two teams, giving each team half of the cards—in a stack, face down. Select a representative from each of the two teams to sit at a table (or stand at the overhead projector or lectern) in the front of your room. Set the clock for one minute, or two minutes if you feel they need more time. At the word "go," one representative flips over the first card and gives clues to her teammates. Her goal is to get them to say the vocabulary term at the top of the card without using any of the related terms listed below the line or any portion of the vocabulary word. However, if an audience member of the team says one of the taboo words listed on the card, the representative can then use that word in her clues toward the vocabulary word. She may not use any gestures, spellings, sound effects, or rhymes in her clues. Here's an example:

The vocabulary word is "adverb." The Taboo words are "adjective," "degree," "manner," "modify," "place," "speech," "time," and "verb." The representative might say: "This is a type of word. It changes other words and words like itself. Those words are often made by putting –ly on the end. It tells us how something was done."

The team members can call out the answer at any time. If the team members guess correctly, their representative puts that card to one side, picks up the next one from the pile, and starts giving new clues. The process continues until time is called.

The opposing team's representative is responsible for using the buzzer (or squeaky toy) to indicate an infraction of the rules—the clue-giver accidentally using a taboo word or a portion of the vocabulary term. The clue-giver must forfeit the card and the opposing team gets a point for each card forfeited. If the clue-giving team's representative can't communicate a vocabulary term successfully to her team, she can pass on the card, but the opposing team also gets a point for each card passed.

Keep playing until both teams have had the same number of opportunities to give clues or until time runs out. For fun, throw in a few cards relating to students' interests, such as favorite books, current events, movies, or sports teams.

Variations and Extended Applications

This technique is easy to vary according to the needs of your students. The more taboo words on each card you include, the more difficult the game, as students have to look beyond the easier descriptions and think harder about how to express the concept.

Once you've played the game with students, they'll have a better idea of the game and how to make the cards. Invite them to make their own deck of Taboo cards using the vocabulary terms and concepts of the current unit of study. Don't forget to have students put their cards in rubber bands or plastic bags and turn the cards in to you a day or two in advance. Go through them, assessing students understanding of the topics.

Test Notes

Most of us have had teachers or professors who would let us "use notes" during an exam—as long as the notes were on one side of a standard, 3-by-5-inch index card. Remember how this went? The day before, we would feverishly write everything—in tiny print on the card, with little lines sectioning topics from one another. (See Figure 28.) If something was going to be too long, we encapsulated it so it would fit. Because it didn't all fit, we decided to write simple mnemonics to help us remember material. We felt we didn't need to spend any time studying because we had the security blanket of the index card. Later, of course, we realized that we'd been tricked. Making the card forced us to think about the material and to summarize it; we had been studying and learning all along.

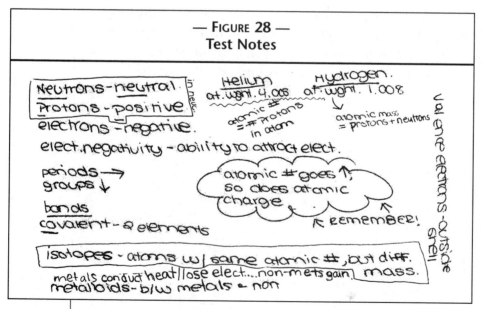

— FIGURE 28 —
Test Notes

Basic Sequence

One or two weeks before a big test, announce to your students that they'll be able to use notes during the test as long as those notes fit on to a standard index card. Hand out the cards and keep a stack of additional cards available. Reassure the students that yes, they can write as small as they like, and yes, they can include anything that will help them ace the test: definitions, names, dates, formulas, diagrams, and so on. If you think students might copy each other's cards, ask them to complete the cards in class, then store the cards for them until test day.

Variations and Extended Applications

Jack Berckemeyer, the assistant executive director of the National Middle School Association, tells the story of how, about two weeks ahead of a major test, he announced to students that he would allow them to create up to four pages of notes to use during the test. The students were all excited. Four pages! Plenty of space to write everything, including major portions of the textbook, in tiny print. A few days later and after everyone had written their notes, Jack announced that a parent had found out about the test notes, and she complained that it seemed like cheating to her. In deference to her, then, he had to cut back the size of the test notes to one side of one sheet of paper. The students groaned, but not too loudly because that still left them with lots of space. They reworked their notes, cutting some things, encapsulating others.

A few days before the test, Jack went back to the class in mock disappointment, claiming that the principal had gotten wind of what he was doing and requested that it be no more than one side of an index card. Again the students groaned, but they recorded all they could on the card and discarded their one sheet of notes. Now they had copied and summarized their notes three times. They muttered the material in their sleep. They knew it backward and forward, grouped and ungrouped, as acronyms and not. On the day of the test, they put their cards at the top of the desk and never used them.

Think-Pair-Share

This classic summarization method is more of a procedure than a specific prompt. Think-Pair-Share can be used repeatedly throughout the year as it gets students interacting substantively with the topic. Because the first step (Think) is an individual activity, it's not threatening. That emotional safety is maintained in the second step (Pair) because individuals share with only one other person. When it comes time to perform step three (Share) with the whole class, what the students are sharing is usually just one or two ideas or a general report of the conversation, not any one student's specific contribution.

Basic Sequence

Ask your students to reflect on a topic using art, writing, or by just sitting quietly. It works best to give them a structure, however, instead of leaving them to their own devices. Giving students specific prompts keeps them focused on the topic. The prompts can be as simple as "Record at least five new concepts you've learned today," "Identify three ways this affects citizens in our community," or "How is this analogous to _____?"

After a few minutes of brainstorming possible responses, ask students to pair up (or assign pairs) and to share their responses. Invite partners to ask each other clarifying and follow-up questions. (This technique is easily taught by modeling a couple of partner interactions for the class using one of your students as your partner.) Stress to students that the purpose of this exchange is to help them revise and tighten their original ideas.

The next step is for the students to share these ideas with the rest of their classmates. There are several ways they might do this.

- Each partner shares one interesting response made by his or her partner.

- The partners come up with one or two observations they'd like to make.

- The partners create a product that expresses what they shared. The product should be decided by the teacher and can be a form of artwork, a performance, a short paper, or anything else.

- The partners post their best thinking electronically in an online class portfolio, Web site, or registry.

- The partners take what they discussed and apply that information to a new prompt posted by the teacher. Their response to the second prompt is posted for all classmates to see.

Variations and Extended Applications

Because it's short and easy to conduct, Think-Pair-Share has been a favorite among teachers for years. The activity ensures that everyone is summarizing and interacting with the information, not just the three or four students on whom the teacher calls during a class discussion. Think-pair-share can last as long as necessary, from six minutes to half a class period. I've used it several times a month in some school years, and it's successful every time.

Traditional Rules-Based Summaries

Straightforward summaries, based on a set of formal summarization rules, can be highly effective for students. You should conduct such summarization on a regular basis, but not to the exclusion of alternative formats. Traditional summaries are often very subjective and creative, so make sure you use the summary evaluation suggestions listed in Part 2.

Marzano and his colleagues (2001) had it right when they reported that basic summarization boils down to three steps: deleting information, substituting information, and keeping information. Knowing what to delete, substitute, and keep as we summarize will stem from the parameters outlined in Part 2: a student's prior knowledge, the structures of the text or experience, the priming of the student's mind, the breadth of students' vocabulary, the setting of a purpose, or the determination of how information is already chunked, to name a few.

To develop students' ability to decide what to delete, substitute, and keep, you should give them repeated models and practice opportunities. Be overt about the process. Put up newsprint or an overhead for your students to read and summarize; then think aloud for them as you summarize a portion of it while playing the role of a student:

"Now, what do I need to take out? Well, this sentence repeats what that sentence says, so I'll cross it out [place a line through it]. This part is just a wordy description [place a line through it], but this part is key [circle it]. My teacher said this would be a subset of that, so I'll need to keep it but delete this other material over here because it was not mentioned by my teacher as necessary for the project we're doing [place a line through it]."

Marzano and colleagues also mentioned rules-based summarization as did Browne, Campione, and Day (1981). That approach breaks down effective summarization to its basic steps. Summarization is no longer some mysterious skill other students have; it is accessible to all students, even those who struggle with the process.

Basic Sequence

Traditional or rules-based summarizations consist of four steps.

1. Draw a line through anything that seems trivial or frivolous, such as adjectives, side comments, similar examples, and transition words (although the summarizer should pay attention to the logic imposed by carefully selected transition words).

2. Draw a line through anything that is redundant or repetitive. The author might be trying to elaborate, but if we get his point with the first example or explanation, we don't need the rest of the text to encapsulate his message.

3. Replace specific terms with general terms. For example, if the original text lists "flies, honeybees, mosquitoes, and moths," the student might substitute "flying insects."

4. Finally, determine a good topic sentence for the material. Just remember that every topic sentence has two parts: the subject and the author's claim about it. "Civil rights" is not a topic sentence; it's a subject. "Civil rights are negatively affected by homeland security laws" is a topic sentence.

Students can easily remember these four steps by using the term "T–RG–TS" or TARGETS.

T—*Trivia* (Remove trivial material.)

R—*Redundancies* (Remove redundant or repetitive information.)

G—*Generalize* (Replace specifics or lists with general terms and phrases.)

TS—*Topic Sentence* (Determine the topic sentence, which is the subject plus the author's claim about the subject.)

When it's time to summarize, students will identify the target (purpose) for learning the material, and then will conduct the TARGETS summarization. Students won't forget the steps with this mnemonic device.

Even when students do more innovative summaries, the steps of traditional, rules-based summaries are very useful, so they're worth learning and periodically reviewing. Students will improve their summarization competency as they mature and as they have opportunities to practice. Feedback is paramount, however. Students will understand and use traditional summarization if they are provided time to analyze what worked and what didn't.

Variations and Extended Applications

It might be easier for students to remember those first three steps we mentioned earlier: delete, substitute, keep. Help students identify a mnemonic for these steps. The starting letters are *d*, *s*, and *k*, written in any order: *K*ids *S*ummarize *D*aily? *S*tudents *D*are to *K*now? *S*ay, *D*o, *K*now? (This last one is a great sequence for learning things!) The important thing is for students to design the memory device themselves.

This summary technique won't work well for all students if you use it only once or twice. Practice with it is essential. Count on much more effective summarizations the third or fourth time students use this process. Don't forget, too, that those practices are best done by students individually or in groups at their seats, or by students modeling think-alouds for the class—not for the teacher. It's worth it to work with a student leader a day or two ahead of time so he or she can provide an accurate rendering of the skill for classmates.

Triads

In basketball, once a player with the ball stops dribbling, he can't start again. He is rooted to that spot on the court, required to pass the ball to a teammate or to take a shot at the hoop. The most he can do is pivot: one foot stays anchored while the other steps in any direction. It's a disadvantageous position; there's a good chance the other team will steal the ball.

The same thing happens when you as the teacher act as the pivot man or woman in a class discussion: you can get stuck and hold up the game. In the traditional "pivot" position, the teacher processes the meaning of what students contribute to class discussions and summarizations. The teacher asks a question of a student; the student responds, and the teacher clarifies, confronts, encapsulates, helps others understand, and personally responds to what the student contributes. The problem, of course, is that students, not the teacher, should be clarifying, confronting, encapsulating, helping others to understand, and responding to classmates and material. The one who is doing the responding is doing the learning. The one who sits passively watching another respond is gaining little, if any, knowledge. Triads and similar strategies provide ways to change that classroom habit.

Basic Sequence

When it's time for the class to review, summarize, or discuss information to be learned, begin by asking a student a question. This student will be the first of three (a triad) who will engage orally with the content. Other students may be concerned about whether or not they will be called on, so they are engaged as well. After the first student responds to your question, keep your own reaction to the student's contribution silent. Instead, redirect the first student's response to a second student by saying "[Name of second student], please give evidence to support or refute what [name of first student] just said." When you do this, you're a facilitator, and the students making sense of the responses and the content are the ones learning.

The second student gives supporting details or a rationale denying or supporting some or all of what the first student said. You then call on a third student to evaluate the merits of the second student's claim and evidence about the first student's response.

Now, return to the first student, and ask that student to make a final rebuttal or comment on what the classmates said. As you move from student to student, the triad can't let their mental guard down. The students' minds are energized and stimulated after each prompt. When you pose the question, students are thinking about their answers—and about whether you will decide to call on them, though some are probably in silent prayer that you won't. Classmates can't rest after you call on the first student because they realize you might call on them to provide evidence for or against that student's claim. They can't rest and tune out after the second student is called on either, for the same reason. The first student can't rest or tune out because you are coming back in a moment for a final comment. If we have a culture of such exchanges, students' cognitive centers will operate at a higher level of alertness. They're learning and we're teaching.

We teachers have three roles in triads: (1) to make sure nothing inaccurate is communicated, (2) to call on the next student to respond, and (3) to pose the first question and some of the follow-up questions that come to mind. We can correct misinformation with leading questions that ask students to reexamine their claims or conclusions before proceeding. Then we can turn over the prompting (questioning) to students after they get the idea. Imagine the inspired teaching and learning that occur when students conduct their own triads—and they will, given good modeling and time to reflect on the experience.

Variations and Extended Applications

Not every summarization discussion lends itself to triads, but we can take the idea and adapt it. For example, one student solves a math problem in front of the class, the second student determines whether or not there are any mistakes, and the third student declares whether or not the second student's analysis is correct. In a music, foreign language, or drama class, the triad works the same. The point is to increase the number of students who interact with the material and to maximize the students', not the teacher's, processing of what is experienced. Get your students talking and making sense of concepts and skills. If we teachers process the content and skills, students' learning fades. Suddenly, the month-old cafeteria lunch menu on the far wall is more fascinating than the current lesson.

Increasing the use of triads to summarize material may seem risky at first because students will talk more, and you can't always be sure of what they'll say. You'll have more control of the learning and behavior, however, because you're appealing to the brain's social interaction needs. You're the one facilitating every step. It's worth the risk. Let the students teach you how to do it.

Unique Summarization Assignments

Those of us who teach more than 32 students per day can attest to the maturity it takes to buckle down and grade the 131st student's summarization assignment, which is exactly like the 130th student's assignment, which is exactly like the 129th student's assignment and the previous 128 students' assignments. But relief is in sight. Varying the manner in which students interact with information can lead to two amazing outcomes: Teachers enjoy assessing multiple students' responses, and students create innovative responses that surpass what they could have achieved otherwise.

Basic Sequence

Each suggestion in this technique requires students to review and communicate concepts, facts, and skills in a particular format for a particular audience. The summaries must also be accurate and complete. They can be done after any learning experience—art activity, demonstration, field trip, lecture, reading, simulation, skill development, or video—or after one or two lessons or a large unit.

Doing one of these alternative formats often requires rigor, mental dexterity, and expertise beyond what is required in more traditional assignments, such as "define the bold-faced words" or "write a paragraph explaining the top three characteristics of _____." For example, if I ask students to create a menu for a music-themed restaurant, I might find something like this in the section titled "Side Dishes":

Pianissimo Potatoes—Potatoes so soft, you'll whisper for hours after eating them. Be sure to top them with *Forte Figs* to increase vocal strength.

As we evaluate this example, we see that the student spelled and defined the terms, *pianissimo* and *forte*, correctly. His manipulation of the information into this format, however, helped him internalize the content in ways other methods couldn't achieve. He had to think differently about pianissimo and forte.

Students do not need to be identified as gifted to benefit from doing these alternative methods. Sure, there will be students who take ideas farther than others; encourage them to do so. All students, however, learn well when engaged with content in a compelling, creative manner. Imagine the immense amount of information that would be included and the interesting things students would produce when asked to create any of the following:

- A comic strip about the mantissa (the decimal-fraction part of a logarithm)

- A mysterious, yet accurate, archeological map concerning the quadratic formula

- A field guide to the asymptotes of a hyperbola (the diagonals of the rectangle formed by the lines $x = a$, $x = -a$, $y = b$, and $y = -b$ in the hyperbola: x squared over a squared $-y$ squared over b squared)

- A coloring book about Amendments 1, 2, 3, 4, and 10 to the U.S. Constitution

- A rap song that expresses the order of presidential succession

- A grocery list for taiga biomes

- A mural that accurately expresses the checks and balances among our federal government's three branches: judicial, legislative, and executive

- A sculpture or mobile that teaches observers about latitude and longitude

- A court transcript from Othello's murder trial.

- A pop-up book on liquid and dry measures

- A soap opera about valence among chemical elements

- A "Wanted: Dead or Alive" poster using prepositions: "He was last seen in the Over Hill 'n' Dale Saloon, *at* the table, *in* the dark, *under* close scrutiny *of* other scalawags."

Variations and Extended Applications

If you're just starting out, Figure 29 contains a plethora of possible alternative summarization activities.

— FIGURE 29 —
Unique Summarization Ideas

Artistic and Visual
Book jackets
Bulletin boards
Bumper stickers
Calendars
Captions
CD covers
Cereal boxes
Certificates
Coloring books
Comic books
Comic strips
Commercials
Flipbooks
Graffiti
Hieroglyphics
Illustrated folktales and legends
Maps
Menus
Movie posters
Murals
Museum maps and tour guides
Pamphlets
Personal narrative mobiles
Pictographs
Picture books
Play programs
Pop-up books
Post cards
PowerPoint presentations
Puppet shows
Rubrics
Science fiction sketches
Sculpture
Travel brochures
Travel posters
Wanted posters

Aural and Oral
Commercials
Comparisons
Conversations
Inauguration speeches
Interviews
Movie critiques
Odes
Oral histories
Persuasive essays
Poetry
Poetry readings
Radio plays
Rebuttals
Satires and spoofs
Sequels and prequels
Sermons
Songs and raps
Speeches
Wedding vows

Civic and Legal
Certificates
Constitutions
Contracts
Fortunes
Inauguration speeches
Job applications
Police reports
Protest letters
Rebuttals
Resumes
Stockholder's meeting
   presentations
Trial transcriptions
Wills

Computer-based and Electronic
Amazon.com recommendations
Codes
E-magazines
Job applications
Manuals
PowerPoint presentations
Spreadsheets
Telegrams
Web sites

Geographic and Travel-Focused
Maps
Museum maps and tour guides
Travel brochures
Travel posters

Historical
Almanac entries
Autobiographies
Biographies
Constitutions
Diaries
Family trees
Folktales, legends, and myths
Headlines
Hieroglyphics
Historical fiction
Inauguration speeches
Museum maps and tour guides
Newspapers
Oral histories
Pictographs
Slogans
Time lines

— FIGURE 29 —
Unique Summarization Ideas   *(continued)*

Musical
Musical scores
Odes
Requiems
Songs and raps

Performance-Based and Physical
Character sketches
Commercials
Games
Jokes and riddles
Monologues
Persuasive essays
Poetry readings
Puppet shows
Radio plays
Recipes
Satires and spoofs
Science fiction sketches
Scripts
Sequels and prequels
Soap operas

Scientific
Codes
Comparisons
Evaluations
Field guides
How-to books
Informal and formal observations
Information reports
Lab instructions
Manuals
Rubrics
Schedules
Science fiction sketches
Spreadsheets
Surveys
Weather forecasts

Written
Advice columns
Almanac entries
Alphabet books
Animal stories
Annotated catalogs
Autobiographies
Biographies
Book jackets
Bumper stickers
Captions
Cereal boxes
Certificates
Character sketches
Choose-your-own-adventure stories
Coloring books
Comic books
Comic strips
Commercials
Constitutions
Contracts
Diaries
Definitions
E-mails (print outs)
Epilogues
Epithets
Evaluations
Field guides
Flipbooks
Folktales, legends, and myths
Graffiti
Grocery lists
Headlines
Historical fiction
How-to books
Instant Messages (print outs)
Inauguration speech
Indices
Job applications
Jokes and riddles

Journals
Letters
Magazines
Menus
Metaphors
Mini-textbooks
Monologues
Movie critiques
Museum maps and tour guides
Mystery stories
Picture books
Play programs
PowerPoint presentations
Newspapers
Odes
Pamphlets
Persuasive essays
Poetry
Pop-up books
Post cards
Protest letters
Rebuttals
Recipes
Requiems
Romances
Satires and spoofs
Science fiction sketches
Scripts
Sequels and prequels
Sermons
Scary stories
Slogans
Soap operas
Speeches
Sports accounts
Stockholder's meeting presentation
Surveys
Telegrams
Thank you notes
Travel brochure
Wedding vows
Yellow pages

As a teacher, you don't have to be an expert on any of the suggested formats, just on the content and on your students. You are a facilitator and must trust your students to rise to the challenge. Offer them only three to five choices that are appropriate for what you're teaching, not the whole list. Add your own ideas to ones listed here as you think of them. Give your students a chance to stretch their minds, and give your teaching practice fresh energy in the classroom by using alternative summarization formats in your lessons.

I had to explain myself to the community for a couple of weeks one year when I was teaching systems of the body and I told students they could summarize their learning by making a pop-up book. I was teaching every system of the body, if you get my drift, and some students took advantage of the opportunity to . . . well, uh, . . . demonstrate the pop-up nature of the one system in particular.

Verbs? Change Them!

Sometimes your summarization prompts will fail to motivate your students. Maybe the prompts have gotten stale. Even we'd get bored writing to the same "compare this with that" or "identify five ways that this caused that" prompts ourselves, and we're supposedly passionate about our subjects. Breathe new life into your student assignments by changing the action verbs of your summarization prompts.

Compare the following prompts:

Prompt 1: Describe Andrew Johnson's and Abraham Lincoln's different approaches to leading the country during troubled times.

Prompt 2: Rank the following government policies in order of importance as Andrew Johnson would rank them. Then explain how the rankings would be different if Abraham Lincoln were making them. Five government policies will be listed.

The first prompt just asks students to report information. The response doesn't require much thought and it could almost be done as a cut-and-paste off the Internet. That approach echoes information and requires students only to record the information in acceptable sentences in a logical order. Plagiarism and apathy lurk nearby.

The second prompt, however, requires students to use the information to draw conclusions. The rankings are debatable, subject to a student's interpretations. The assignment raises the student's anxiety level a bit: "Can I justify this policy as number one for Johnson, or should it be number two?" a student reasons. "Let me check my notes and think about this carefully." In short, the second prompt is more engaging, and thus, more memorable. The biggest change was the verb, as it changed from "describe" to "rank."

Basic Sequence

Write down what you want students to summarize: how the moon affects the Earth, for example. The next step is to consider if you should ask students to respond to a basic prompt ("What effect does the moon have on the Earth?") or if you should do something more with the prompt.

There are plenty of reasons to stick with the straightforward, direct question, so don't discount it. Some students or situations call for keeping the prompts simple. But if you did so each time, your students would lose interest over the long haul. They would also have very little opportunity to grow intellectually, and their assignments would be tedious to assess. Err on the side of balance, and provide a mixture of both simple and complex prompts.

In this example, let's consider using this prompt: "Imagine an Earth that never had a moon. How would it be different?" After you've considered several options, evaluate whether or not your prompt with the new action verb ("Imagine") requires students to review the material as you intended them to review it. Sometimes action verbs take lessons in directions that don't really address your goals, so analyze the verb you select.

If your prompt maintains the focus on the content that you want students to summarize, keep it. Because ownership is a powerful motivator, I sometimes like to generate multiple prompts and let students choose the one to which they will respond. Of course, all the prompt options must require students to focus on the same content.

Figure 30 lists action verbs that invite the student to interact more with content than to merely "describe" or "list."

— FIGURE 30 —
Verb Suggestions

Analyze . . .	Contrast . . .	Find support for . . .	Predict . . .
Argue against . . .	Create . . .	Formulate . . .	Rank . . .
Argue for . . .	Criticize . . .	Identify . . .	Recommend . . .
Assess . . .	Critique . . .	Imagine . . .	Retell . . .
Blend . . .	Decide between . . .	Infer . . .	Revise . . .
Categorize . . .	Deduce . . .	Interpret . . .	Show . . .
Choose . . .	Defend . . .	Interview . . .	Simplify . . .
Classify . . .	Develop . . .	Invent . . .	Suppose . . .
Combine . . .	Devise . . .	Justify . . .	Why did . . .
Compare . . .	Evaluate . . .	Modify . . .	
Compose . . .	Expand . . .	Organize . . .	
Construct . . .	Explain . . .	Plan . . .	

Variations and Extended Applications

Imagine the wealth of information if students were asked to summarize by doing the following:

- Blend the two concepts into one unifying idea.

- Compose a ballad about the cautious Massasoit tribe coming to dinner with Governor Bradford and his colony in 1621.

- Interpret the Internet for Amazonian inhabitants who have never lived with electricity, let alone a computer.

- Argue for and against democracy as a healthy way to build a country, and provide at least two arguments for each position.

- Classify the Greek gods and goddesses according to three different criteria.

- Predict the limiting factors for this habitat 25 years from now.

- Retell a fairy tale of your choosing with one of the following concepts as its central theme: (1) making healthy decisions, (2) using teamwork, (3) taking positive risks, or (4) explaining "If you're not a part of the solution, you're a part of the problem."

A teacher's job is not just to present materials for building knowledge. He or she must also provide the spark if it's not there. Changing the action verb is a great way to increase the quality of our summarization prompts. Even better, it ignites the interest and enhances competence in students who might be adrift. You can keep all your students engaged with substance by raising the complexity of your summarization prompts.

Word Splash

Walk to the front of your classroom at the start of your lesson carrying a bucket of vocabulary terms written on strips of poster board. Upon reaching the front, trip "accidentally" on something and spill the bucket's contents. Look frustrated and worried. Ask for volunteers to help you put the words back in proper order for the day's lesson. Tell the volunteers to post the terms on the front chalkboard or wall (magnetic tape, masking tape, or plastic-tack will work) in proper order. More than likely, the words will be posted at angles without a lot of logic. Ask your students to postulate some possible connections among the randomly assembled words as they say the words aloud. Your students will be hooked, and their brains will be primed for learning.

Word Splash is a fully formed summarization experience. Although it opens with a "hook" and priming of the brain, its real power comes after the lesson, when students return to the pre-learning activity to make sense of it using their new insights.

Basic Sequence

Identify the content you want students to know and make a list of key vocabulary words and concepts associated with the content. The terms can be new words or commonly known words, but they must be purposeful for the day's lesson. You can use the individual slip-of-paper method I've discussed, or just "splash" those words across a sheet of paper by writing them at cockeyed angles all over the sheet, as shown in Figure 31. Another option is to provide the words in a little envelope for every desk cluster or table group.

Now ask your students to help you put the words and phrases in logical order. You'll find that students often make wild connections, especially if the material is new and they have no frame of reference. Once the groups finish, ask them to share their thinking. Note their varied and occasionally entertaining interpretations. Then ask your students to zero in on what it is they're going to study and what they will be looking for as they read or learn.

Pass out the reading material, conduct your lesson, do your demonstration, watch the video, or whatever else you were going to do to teach the material. When the lesson is complete, ask the students to go back to the words splashed on their papers or desks. Working as a group, their task is to place the words in a logical order that will create a summary of the material they just learned. The arrangement must be accurate and complete. Each group will mix and match terms, physically moving them around the page or desktop. They will discuss what belongs with what and what should be moved to the next sentence.

— FIGURE 31 —
Word Splash Sample

After they have the words arranged, ask them to fill in around the terms with phrases and transitions so they create full sentences and, finally, a well-constructed paragraph or two. Before asking the groups to share their paragraphs, have them revisit the lesson or reading so they make sure that their summary incorporates all they learned, as well as that it is accurate, complete, and clear.

After the groups are done, ask them to share their rendering of the information for a class critique. As each group presents, the other groups evaluate the accuracy, completeness, and clarity of the presenting group's summary. For instance, if you have five groups, the whole class will listen to five different summaries, critiquing them all. By the time the critiques are over, students will know the information very well. Ask the class to vote on the best summary, and have that one photocopied for the whole class, if possible.

Take the time to debrief your students. Was their initial understanding correct? If not, what changed their minds? If it was correct, what background did they have before the lesson that enabled them to make successful connections among the words?

Variations and Extended Applications

Although I've encountered word splashes in multiple formats in many school district guides on instruction, the activity was originally designed by W. Dorsey Hammond, now heading The Seidel School of Education at Salisbury University in Salisbury, Maryland. I've used it in five different subjects with great success.

There is one caution to keep in mind when using a word splash. Because people remember best what we experience first, you don't want to spend too much time on the word-play portion of process, where students are generating their creative conclusions. Let them play a bit, creating a sense of wonder and purpose, but then move fairly quickly into the real content. If you keep things moving, students won't hold on to the early misconceptions and they'll be grounded for the learning that lies ahead.

Conclusion

Most of the techniques in this book are malleable; they can be made shorter or longer, involve fine and performing arts or not, and be completed in written, oral, and physical forms. Because the majority of teachers are now aware that our students are "smart" in different ways and varied in how they learn best, we need to respond to that knowledge by incorporating multiple and varied summary experiences in our lessons. Rather than being a burden, using these experiences breathes new life into teaching practice and effectiveness. Students enjoy the variety, creativity, and structure, and we enjoy students' diverse and substantive responses as we evaluate their work. Our students achieve more, and we rediscover why we entered the profession.

Some of these summarization techniques are more elaborate than others, but they all do the same thing: enable students to distill essence and process or structure it for long-term memory. At each turn, long-term memory is what we're about as teachers. Mark Twain cautioned us that "Teaching is not telling. If it was, we'd all be so smart we couldn't stand ourselves." What teachers present to students doesn't matter in the big scheme of things; it's what students carry forward after their time with us that counts. The learning that students take with them at the end of the school year is our true testimony as professionals, as a school district, and as a community. With so much at stake, we can't settle for just presenting curriculum and leaving it to the students to learn it whatever way they can. We have to give them the tools and inclination to learn the material. Summarization is one way to do that; regardless of grade level or subject matter, it's one of the surest ways to improve student learning.

Use the techniques in this book to develop your students' summarization savvy and as launching points for your own ideas. Feel free to modify directions or change the rules in order to respond best to student needs.

You can take these ideas and make them better. If you get a chance, share your enhancements and alternative approaches with the rest of us via the Web, a magazine article, a book, or a conference workshop. First-year teachers to seasoned veterans, we're waiting for your wisdom.

Appendix

Sample Texts
and Summarization
Practice Activities

THIS APPENDIX INCLUDES A COLLECTION OF ORIGINAL TEXT EXCERPTS AND THREE WORKSHEETS WITH PROMPTS FOR SUMMARIZATION PRACTICE ACTIVITIES. Prompts are keyed to each original text's letter reference and, when the text has multiple paragraphs, its internal number references. Feel free to photocopy this appendix and use the activities in your own class or as catalysts for your own creations.

Although the samples here are necessarily written text, remember that students should summarize information presented in all sorts of formats. As you teach students to summarize and to interact with their learning, use demonstrations, field trips, videos, Web sites, and experiential learning as the original text. The same summarizing principles apply no matter what the source.

A. The Gettysburg Address (1863)

Executive Mansion,
Washington, 1863.

[1] Four score and seven years ago our fathers brought forth on this continent, a new nation, conceived in Liberty, and dedicated to the
proposition that all men are created equal.

[2] Now we are engaged in a great civil war, testing whether that nation,
or any nation so conceived and so dedicated, can long endure. We
are met on a great battle-field of that war. We have come to dedicate
a portion of that field, as a final resting place for those who here gave
their lives that the nation might live. It is altogether fitting and
proper that we should do this.

[3] But, in a larger sense, we can not dedicate—we can not consecrate—
we can not hallow—this ground. The brave men, living and dead,
who struggled here, have consecrated it, far above our poor power to
add or detract. The world will little note, nor long remember what
we say here, but it can never forget what they did here. It is for us
the living, rather, to be dedicated here to the unfinished work which
they who fought here have thus far so nobly advanced. It is rather
for us to be here dedicated to the great task remaining before us—
that from these honored dead we take increased devotion to that
cause for which they gave the last full measure of devotion—that we
here highly resolve these dead shall not have died in vain—that this
nation, under God, shall have a new birth of freedom—and that government of the people, by the people, for the people, shall not perish
from the earth.

B. Letter from Abraham Lincoln to Mrs. Bixby (1864)

Executive Mansion,
Washington
November 21, 1864

Mrs. Bixby,
Boston, Massachusetts

Dear Madam:

I have been shown in the files of the War Department a statement of the Adjutant-General of Massachusetts that you are the mother of five sons who have died gloriously on the field of battle. I feel how weak and fruitless must be any word of mine which should attempt to beguile you from the grief of a loss so overwhelming. But I cannot refrain from tendering to you the consolation that may be found in the thanks of the Republic they died to save. I pray that our Heavenly Father may assuage the anguish of your bereavement, and leave you only the cherished memory of the loved and lost, and the solemn pride that must be yours to have laid so costly a sacrifice upon the altar of freedom.

Yours very sincerely and respectfully,
Abraham Lincoln

C. Humorous Business Letter

Sweettooth Butterworth
1234 Maple Avenue
Pile o' Pancakes, VA 20171
February 30, 2009

Mr. Jim Nasium
12341234 Exercise Way
Physical Education Corporation
Sweatsville, NC 10001

Dear Mr. Nasium:

[1] I'm writing to complain about a portable basketball hoop, back-board, and pole I purchased from your company recently. It's not acceptable, and I would like my money back.

[2] Every time I shoot a basketball toward it, the pole swivels one foot to the side, which moves the rim out from under the approaching ball. If I adjust my throw to account for the basketball rim's move-ment, the hoop just swivels to the other side. When I try to run up and do a slam dunk, the net, backboard, rim, and pole just get up and move. I know I ordered a portable basketball net, but this is ridiculous. Try explaining this to the neighbors! I can't practice my shots, and, frankly, I'm feeling rejected by a basketball hoop. I'm not sure if the net is being mean or just being shy, but as far as I'm concerned, it's broken. My friend Harry Potter just smiles when he watches me play. He seems to know something about these hoops, but I don't, and I want restitution.

[3] Please restore my sanity and self-esteem by giving me a complete refund for this bad product. Please send me a check for $4,236.79. I would also accept a replacement basketball hoop, one with a much calmer temperament. Thank you for any consid-eration you can give me on this matter.

Blue Skies and Peace to the World,

Sweettooth Butterworth

Sweettooth Butterworth

D. Narrative Description

Moisture dripped from the large banana leaves and fell on the damp soil. Every few minutes, he had to peel his shirt away from his stomach. The sweat on his face gathered in great droplets and rolled downward, following the curve of his eyebrows and cheekbones. Breathing was like sucking mud through a straw—he hoped at least once he'd get a pocket of clear, fresh air, but each inhale was the same—wet and full of mildew. Hiking up the steep incline toward the Mayan ruins turned his leg muscles to well-boiled noodles. He stopped and unfolded the map for the seventh time, noting his fingers were as wrinkled as they were after a long swim.

E. Comment on Exclamation Points
by Lewis Thomas (1979)

Exclamation points are the most irritating of all. Look! they say, look at what I just said! How amazing is my thought! It is like being forced to watch someone else's small child jumping up and down crazily in the center of the living room shouting to attract attention.

From Thomas, L. *The medusa and the snail: More notes of a biology watcher* (reprint edition). New York: Penguin Books, 1995, p. 127.

F. Comment on Writing by Huckleberry Finn (per Mark Twain, 1884)

And so there ain't nothing more to write about, and I am rotten glad of it, because if I'd 'a' knowed what a trouble it was to make a book, I wouldn't 'a' tackled it, and ain't a-going to no more.

G. Excerpt from *The Pale Blue Dot,* by Carl Sagan (1994)

Our planet is a lonely speck in the great enveloping cosmic dark. In our obscurity, in all this vastness, there is no hint that help will come from elsewhere to save us from ourselves. . . . It has been said that astronomy is a humbling and character-building experience. There is perhaps no better demonstration of the folly of human conceits than this distant image of our tiny world. To me, it underscores our responsibility to deal more kindly with one another, and to preserve and cherish that pale blue dot, the only home we've ever known.

From Sagan, C. *Pale blue dot: A vision of the human future in space* (paperback edition). New York: Ballantine Books, 1997, p. 7.

H. "The Charge of the Light Brigade"
by Alfred, Lord Tennyson (1854)

Half a league, half a league,
Half a league onward,
All in the valley of Death
Rode the six hundred.
"Forward, the Light Brigade!
Charge for the guns!" he said:
Into the valley of Death
Rode the six hundred.

"Forward, the Light Brigade!"
Was there a man dismay'd?
Not tho' the soldier knew
Some one had blunder'd:
Theirs not to make reply,
Theirs not to reason why,
Theirs but to do and die
Into the valley of Death
Rode the six hundred.

Cannon to right of them,
Cannon to left of them,
Cannon in front of them
Volley'd and thunder'd;
Storm'd at with shot and shell,
Boldly they rode and well,
Into the jaws of Death,
Into the mouth of Hell
Rode the six hundred.

Flash'd all their sabres bare,
Flash'd as they turn'd in air,
Sabring the gunners there,
Charging an army while
All the world wonder'd:
Plunged in the battery-smoke
Right thro' the line they broke;
Cossack and Russian
Reel'd from the sabre-stroke
Shatter'd and sunder'd.
Then they rode back, but not
Not the six hundred.

Cannon to right of them,
Cannon to left of them,
Cannon behind them
Volley'd and thunder'd;
Storm'd at with shot and shell,
While horse and hero fell,
They that had fought so well
Came thro' the jaws of Death
Back from the mouth of Hell,
All that was left of them,
Left of six hundred.

When can their glory fade?
O the wild charge they made!
All the world wondered.
Honor the charge they made!
Honor the Light Brigade!
Noble six hundred!

I. Description of the Space Shuttle

The three main components of the Space Shuttle are the orbiter, the external tank, and the solid rocket boosters. The Shuttle weighs 4.5 million pounds at launch time and is 184.2 feet tall. It is 78.06 feet across at its wingtips and 122.2 feet long. Each of its three engines produces 470,000 pounds of thrust, and the two solid rocket boosters produce 5.3 million pounds of thrust combined. It can carry up to 65,000 pounds of cargo on one mission.

J. Teacher's Comment on Gangs in Schools

Middle school students usually begin gang involvement by forming "Wannabee" gangs. These are groups of friends who hear about or even witness older adolescent gang activities, then experiment with the less-dangerous aspects of gang life. Middle school students are also recruited directly into the older gangs by older siblings or friends. One of my students told me he was a gang member because the 19-year-old gang leader had a car and hung out with them. When I compared that relationship to a 13-year-old student hanging out with 1st graders, he didn't see anything amiss. "He's got a car, man," he said. "What's the big deal?"

K. Opinion Piece on Teenage Apathy

[1] Teenage apathy is the result of many things. First, teenagers watch too much television. Television is passive, which means it doesn't require any interaction or activity. Teenagers just sit there and soak in the repetitive drivel that passes for entertainment. Parents come into the room to speak with them, and teenagers hang their mouths open and say, "Okay," in a zombie voice. When friends call on the phone, TV teenagers who don't want to be bothered during a show sometimes lie, telling their friends that they don't feel well. Research has proven that students who watch more than six hours of television per week achieve less in school, and most often it's because they claim they're just too bored and tired to do the work.

[2] Another factor in teenage apathy is the lack of exciting things to do in our community. Most activities are for young kids, families, or just adults. There is no hangout for teenagers.

[3] Finally, many teenagers are bored and don't care about school work because they see how hard life is for others, and they wonder—why bother? They need to have enthusiastic adults who show them the way to success in a compelling manner. Teenagers want to know that they make good company, that they have something to contribute, and that they are enjoyable to be around.

[4] Teenagers would care about living, and they would achieve more, if the television were turned off, if our community provided safe and fun teenage hangouts, and if positive adults spent more time with them.

L. Three-Dimensional Solids

3-D Solid	# of Faces	# of Edges	# of Vertices	Comments
Cube	6	12	8	All faces are congruent
Rectangular Prism	6	12	8	Named for the shape of its sides
Triangular Prism	5	9	6	
Pentagonal Prism	7	15	10	
Triangular Pyramid	4	6	4	Named for the shape of its base
Rectangular Pyramid	5	8	5	
Pentagonal Pyramid	6	10	6	
Cone	2	2	1	
Sphere	1	0	0	

M. Book Censorship and *Huckleberry Finn*

[1] People challenge or ban books so they can protect children from difficult or inappropriate ideas or information, or so they can ban others from information that they don't want those people to know or that they think somehow will threaten a government's goals (for example, Nazis burned books during the Holocaust). A book challenge is the attempt to remove or restrict materials on the basis of the objections of a person or group. A banning is the removal of those materials, thereby restricting access by others.

[2] Mark Twain's book, *Huckleberry Finn* is frequently challenged and banned in school systems across America. Writer Jamey Fletcher is frustrated by its misinterpretation and banning. He says, "Even to the present day, we so often condemn books that were written to fight the very things we claim to be fighting. Mark Twain's (Samuel Clemens's) *Huckleberry Finn* is so often cited as being racist, when it was written against slavery and racism."

[3] Much has been said of *Huckleberry Finn's* effect on youth and writing, including an observation from Ernest Hemingway: "All modern American literature comes from one book by Mark Twain called *Huckleberry Finn.* All American writing comes from that. There was nothing before. There has been nothing as good since." *Huckleberry Finn* was banned in some places even when Mark Twain was still living. Twain laughed at this and told his editor that banning the book would sell 25,000 copies for sure. He commented on *Huckleberry Finn's* detractors when he added, "God has not dealt kindly with them in the matter of wisdom."

N. Excerpts from *Hamlet*

Horatio: In what particular thought to work I know not;
But, in the gross and scope of my opinion,
This bodes some strange eruption to our state.
(Act I, Scene 1, lines 67–69)

Polonius: . . . to thine own self be true;
And it must follow, as the night the day,
Thou canst not then be false to any man.
(Act I, Scene 3, lines 78–80)

O. Sports Report

[1] The Grasshopper All-Stars Soccer Team scored the winning goal last Saturday to win the tournament, 5 games to 3. Lynn Marie Tackleberry made the final goal with an assisting setup by Lucy Shinkicker, Melba Nohands, and Jenny Kleetcaker. Coach Rick Clipboarder said the team started off slowly this week, losing three games in a row. "But somehow the girls woke up later in the week," he said. "The whole team rallied yesterday and today to come from behind and show what they were made of. We're all really proud of them."

[2] As part of the celebration, the team will have dinner with the president at the White House in Washington, D.C., on Thursday and then will go on a world tour for nine months, playing exhibition soccer in five different continents. When asked how she felt about the soccer tour, Lynn Marie responded, "What am I going to tell my basketball coach?"

Activity: Determining Topic Sentences

Name: _____ Date: _____

Directions: For each original text identified below, circle the number of all reasonable topic sentences. Then circle the subject and underline the author's claim about it. If none of the options are reasonable topic sentences, circle "None of these."

Original Text: Gettysburg Address (A, 1)

1. Our nation started a new push for freedom.
2. People wanted equality.
3. The people who began our country based it on calls for freedom and equality.
4. Almost 90 years ago, our country began and it was dedicated.
5. None of these.

Original Text: Humorous Business Letter (C, 2)

1. No matter what I do, the basketball net and pole keep moving around, and it's really bothering me.
2. There's something wrong with the basketball net and pole, and I'm not sure what it is.
3. My neighbors are asking questions about my strange basketball net and pole.
4. I want to get my money back.
5. None of these.

Original Text: Narrative Description (D)

1. It's hot and humid.
2. Mayan ruins are located in humid jungles.
3. It had just rained in the jungle.
4. His body was tired and wet from the hiking and humidity.
5. None of these.

Activity: Writing a Topic Sentence

Name: _____ Date:_____

Directions: Write a topic sentence for each of these texts.

1. Original Text: Comment on Exclamation Points by Lewis Thomas (E)
Topic Sentence:

2. Original Text: Comment on Writing by Huckleberry Finn (F)
Topic Sentence:

3. Original Text: Excerpt from *The Pale Blue Dot* by Carl Sagan (G)
Topic Sentence:

4. Original Text: Description of the Space Shuttle (I)
Topic Sentence:

5. Original Text: Teacher's Comment on Gangs in Schools (J)
Topic Sentence:

6. Original Text: Opinion Piece on Teenage Apathy (K, 1)
Topic Sentence:

7. Original Text: Book Censorship and *Huckleberry Finn* (M, 2)
Topic Sentence:

8. Original Text: Sports Report (O)
Topic Sentence:

Activity: Evaluating Summaries

Name: _____ Date: _____

Part I. *Directions:* For each text identified, evaluate the summaries provided. Record your evaluations on a separate sheet of paper. Use the following criteria for successful summaries in your evaluations:

- Does the summary convey the information accurately?

- Is the summary too narrow (limited) or too broad (general)? Does it convey all the important elements? Does it convey too much?

- Would someone else using this summary gain all he or she needed to know to understand the subject?

- If sequence is important, are items in the right order?

- Did the author leave out his or her opinion and just report an undistorted essence of the original content?

- Did he or she paraphrase successfully?

1. Original Text: Letter from Abraham Lincoln to Mrs. Bixby (B)

Summary A: Mrs. Bixby, There is nothing I can say to adequately convey my sorrow at your loss of five sons in battle, but if it helps, know this: They died fighting for freedom and their ideals, and your country is forever thankful for their efforts and your sacrifice. Abraham Lincoln

Summary B: Mrs. Bixby, I was just informed of the loss of your five sons in battle. Please know they died bravely and our country is thankful. Abraham Lincoln. (I think this is an emotional letter all schoolchildren should read.)

Summary C: Mrs. Bixby, You are the mother of five sons who died in battle. My words are weak and useless to convince you from being so sad in a time of such sorrow. I can't help but write, however, to try to help you heal by letting you know the country thanks them for their bravery and sacrifice. I hope God softens your anguish, allowing only loving memories to fill your heart. You have a lot to be proud of, though it's rough right now. You've made the ultimate sacrifice for our country's liberties. Abraham Lincoln

2. Original Text: Humorous Business Letter (C, 3)

Summary A: Please help me by reimbursing me for costs or by replacing the basketball net and pole.

Summary B: Give me back a life by returning all the money I spent on this product and that is $4,236.79. Instead, however, you can send me a replacement basketball net and pole—one that is nicer. I'm grateful for anything you can do.

Summary C: Thank you for listening to my problem. I hope you can help me.

3. Original Text: "The Charge of the Light Brigade" (H)

Summary A: This is a haunting poem. Tennyson deserves great acclaim for lifting this courageous moment from a misled war and so evocatively rendering its drama. He skillfully weaves historical accuracy with strategic literary devices to give the reader not only a sense of being in the battle, but also of appreciating the sacrifices made by the common soldiers who were asked to charge into battle by their inept leaders. The poem stands the test of time as well, serving as a cautionary tale for today's military and business leadership. Reflecting the modern world as well as the era in which it was written is a characteristic of a classic poem. The piece is well-suited for middle and high school courses of study.

Summary B: More than 600 unprepared and simply-armed soldiers marched into battle against a much larger and better fortified battery of enemy forces. They did it even though they knew it was a suicide mission. Their motivation was loyalty and a sense of duty. They trusted their superior officers to know why this had to be done, so they marched into the nightmare. The group found itself completely surrounded by noise, weapons, blood, violence, and death, yet still they battled. In the end, only a fraction of their group returned safely. The poet, Tennyson, asks the world to never forget the valiant effort of these soldiers.

Summary C: The poem uses many literary devices to memorialize the more than 600 soldiers who went into a deadly battle where they were severely outnumbered and suffered dramatic losses. Throughout the poem we find several examples of repetition, allusion, personification, rhythm, onomatopoeia, and alliteration used to evoke a graphic sense of being in the battle and he larger historical context. The poet, Tennyson, also appeals to our senses, vividly portraying the unrelenting physical harm that the soldiers suffered and their emotional anguish stemming from their undeserved trust in their inept leaders. Skillfully crafted, the poem is an evocative depiction of man's nobility rising amidst his fallibility.

Part II. *Directions:* Summarize the Chart of Three-Dimensional Solids **(Original Text L)** in the space below, and ask a classmate or a family member to evaluate how well you did.

Activity: Paraphrasing

Name: _____ Date: _____

Part I. *Directions:* For each text, indicate all reasonable paraphrases. Be prepared to explain why your circled statements demonstrate good paraphrasing technique.

1. Original Text: Excerpts from Hamlet (N)

"In what particular thought to work I know not;
But in the gross and scope of my opinion,
This bodes some strange eruption to our state."

   a. I'm confused.

   b. I'm not sure, but I think the nearby volcano is about to blow lava chunks.

   c. I'm not sure, but whatever it is, it can't be good.

   d. I'm not sure, but I think things around here are about to change dramatically.

2. Original Text: Excerpts from *Hamlet* (N)

". . . to thine own self be true;
And it must follow, as the night the day,
Thou canst not then be false to any man."

   a. We have to be honest with who we really are, and most assuredly, we have to be straight-forward with others.

   b. Don't talk yourself into being something you're not. Just as sure as the sun will come up tomorrow, we can't survive by putting on pretenses.

   c. Be honest with yourself and with others, or you'll never succeed.

   d. Follow your own dreams on a daily basis, and don't lie to anyone.

3. Original Text: Opinion Piece on Teenage Apathy (K)

"Teenagers would care about living, and they would achieve more, if the television was turned off, if our community provided safe and fun teenage hangouts, and if positive adults spent more time with them."

a. Being a teenager is hard. Television, lack of cool places to go, and lack of caring adults make it difficult.

b. Television makes adolescents apathetic. They'd also be happier if there were cool places to gather and if more adults enjoyed their company.

c. If we want adolescents to strive, we have to remove those things that make them apathetic, and we have to provide resources for engagement as well as adult leadership.

d. Teenagers would be concerned for their lives, and they would get better grades in school, if they didn't watch television so much. Our community also has to create safe and enjoyable places to hang out, and we have to find good adults to be involved in teenagers' lives.

Part II. *Directions:* Paraphrase the following statements. Then explain to a classmate or family member why each of your paraphrases is appropriate. Once that classmate or family member has heard your rationale, ask him or her to use the space below to evaluate your success.

1. Original Text: The Gettysburg Address (A)

"But, in a larger sense, we can not dedicate—we can not consecrate—we can not hallow—this ground. The brave men, living and dead, who struggled here, have consecrated it, far above our poor power to add or detract."

Paraphrased:

Reviewer Signature: _____

Is this a successful paraphrasing?   Yes   No   (Circle one)

Please name one characteristic that supports your evaluation:

2. Original Text: Comment on Exclamation Points
by Lewis Thomas (E)

"Exclamation points are the most irritating of all. Look! they say, look at what I just said! How amazing is my thought! It is like being forced to watch someone else's small child jumping up and down crazily in the center of the living room shouting to attract attention."

Paraphrased:

Reviewer Signature: _____

Is this a successful paraphrasing?   Yes   No   (Circle one)

Please name one characteristic that supports your evaluation:

3. Original Text: Excerpt from *The Pale Blue Dot* by Carl Sagan (G)

"It's been said that astronomy is a humbling and, I might add, a character-building experience. To my mind, there is perhaps no better demonstration of the folly of human conceits than this distant image of our tiny world. To me, it underscores our responsibility to deal more kindly and compassionately with one another and to preserve and cherish that pale blue dot, the only home we've ever known."

Paraphrased:

Reviewer Signature: _____

Is this a successful paraphrasing?   Yes   No   (Circle one)

Please name one characteristic that supports your evaluation:

4. Original Text: Description of the Space Shuttle (I)

"The three main components of the Space Shuttle are the orbiter, the external tank, and the solid rocket boosters. The Shuttle weighs 4.5 million pounds at launch time and is 184.2 feet tall. It is 78.06 feet across at its wingtips and 122.2 feet long. Each of its three engines produces 470,000 pounds of thrust, and the two solid rocket boosters produce 5.3 million pounds of thrust combined. It can carry up to 65,000 pounds of cargo on one mission."

Paraphrased:

Reviewer Signature: _____

Is this a successful paraphrasing?   Yes   No   (Circle one)

Please name one characteristic that supports your evaluation:

Resources

Allen, J. (1999). *Words, words, words: Teaching vocabulary in grades 4–12.* York, ME: Stenhouse Publishers.

Armstrong, T. (2000). *Multiple intelligences in the classroom* (2nd ed.). Alexandria, VA: Association for Supervision and Curriculum Development.

Atwell, N. (1990). *Coming to know: Writing to learn in the intermediate grades.* Portsmouth, NH: Heinemann.

Black, H., & Parks, S. (1990). *Organizing thinking: Book II: Graphic organizers.* Pacific Grove, CA: Critical Thinking Books and Software.

Browne, A. L., Campione, J. C., & Day, J. (1981, February). Learning to learn: On training students to learn from texts. *Educational Researcher 10*(2), 14–21.

Buehl, D. (2001). *Classroom strategies for interactive learning* (2nd ed.). Newark, DE: International Reading Association.

Burchers, S., Burchers, B., & Burchers, M. (1996). *Vocabutoons, elementary edition.* Punta Gorda, FL: New Monic Books.

Burke, J. (2001). *Illuminating texts: How to teach students to read the world.* Portsmouth, NH: Heinemann.

Burmark, L. (2001). *Visual literacy: Learn to see, see to learn.* Alexandria, VA: Association for Supervision and Curriculum Development.

Canady, R. L., & Rettig, M. D. (Eds.). (1996). *Teaching in the block: Strategies for engaging active learners.* Larchmont, NY: Eye on Education.

de Bono, E. (1985). *Six thinking hats* (Rev. ed.). Boston: Little, Brown, and Company.

Forsten, C., Grant, J., & Hollas, B. (2003). *Differentiating textbooks: Strategies to improve student comprehension and motivation.* Petersborough, NH: Crystal Springs Books.

Frank, M., Howard, J., & Bullock, K. (1995). *If you're trying to teach kids how to write, you've gotta have this book!* (Rev. ed.). Nashville, TN: Incentive Publications.

Frender, G. (1990). *Learning to learn: Strengthening study skills and brain power.* Nashville, TN: Incentive Publications.

Gardner, H. (1993). *Frames of mind: The theory of multiple intelligences* (10th anniversary ed.). New York: Basic Books.

Glynn, C. (2001). *Learning on their feet: A sourcebook for kinesthetic learning across the curriculum.* Shoreham, VT: Discover Writing Company.

Gordon, W. J. J. (1961). *Synectics, the development of creative capacity.* New York: Harper.

Harvey, S. (1998). *Nonfiction matters: Reading, writing, and research in grades 3–8.* York, ME: Stenhouse Publishers.

Harvey, S., Goudvis, A., & Groves, D. (2001). *Strategies that work: Teaching comprehension to enhance understanding.* York, ME: Stenhouse Publishers.

Hyerle, D. (2000). *A field guide to using visual tools.* Alexandria, VA: Association for Supervision and Curriculum Development.

Hyerle, D. (Ed.). (2004). *Student successes with thinking maps: School-based research, results, and models for achievement using visual tools.* Thousand Oaks, CA: Corwin Press.

Lane, B. (1993). *After the end: Teaching and learning creative revision.* Portsmouth, NH: Heinemann.

Marzano, R. J., Norford, J. S., Paynter, D. E., Pickering, D. J., & Gaddy, B. B. (2001). *A handbook for classroom instruction that works.* Alexandria, VA: Association for Supervision and Curriculum Development.

Marzano, R. J., Pickering, D. J., & Pollock, J. E. (2001). *Classroom instruction that works: Research-based strategies for increasing student achievement.* Alexandria, VA: Association for Supervision and Curriculum Development.

Robb, L. (2000). *Teaching reading in middle school.* New York: Scholastic Professional Books.

Sousa, D. A. (2001a). *How the special needs brain learns.* Thousand Oaks, CA: Corwin Press.

Sousa, D. A. (2001b). *How the brain learns: A classroom teacher's guide.* (2nd ed.). Thousand Oaks, CA: Corwin Press.

Sousa, D. A. (2003). *How the gifted brain learns.* Thousand Oaks, CA: Corwin Press.

Stephens, E. C., & Brown, J. E. (2000). *A handbook of content literacy strategies: 75 practical reading and writing ideas.* Norwood, MA: Christopher-Gordon Publishers.

Strong, R. W., Silver, H. F., Perini, M. J., & Tuculescu, G. M. (2002). *Reading for academic success: Powerful strategies for struggling, average, and advanced readers, grades 7–12.* Thousand Oaks, CA: Corwin Press.

Tovani, C. (2000). *I read it, but I don't get it: Comprehension strategies for adolescent readers.* Portland, ME: Stenhouse Publishers.

Vacca, R. T., & Vacca J. A. L. (2005). *Content area reading: Literacy and learning across the curriculum* (8th ed.). Boston: Pearson/Allyn and Bacon.

Wolfe, P. (2001). *Brain matters: Translating research into classroom practice.* Alexandria, VA: Association for Supervision and Curriculum Development.

Wood, K. D., & Harmon, J. M. (2001). *Strategies for integrating reading and writing in middle and high school classrooms.* Westerville, OH: National Middle School Association.

Zinsser, W. K. (1988). *Writing to learn.* New York: Harper & Row.

Index

Note: An *f* following a page number indicates a figure.

3-2-1 technique, 39–40

Acronyms technique, 41–43. *See also* mnemonics
active listening, 28–29
Advance Organizers technique, 44–45
analogy techniques, 18–19, 64–67, 65–66*f*
Analysis Matrices technique, 46–56, 51–56*f*
anticipation techniques. *See* the brain, priming for learning
artistic/performance summarization techniques. *See* summarization techniques, artistic/performance

Backwards Summaries technique, 57–59
Ball technique, 158–159
Berckemeyer, Jack, 171
Bloom's Taxonomy Summary Cubes, 60–63, 61–62*f*
Body Analogies technique, 18–19, 64–67, 65–66*f*
Body Sculpture technique, 68–72
the brain, priming for learning
    Analysis Matrices, 46, 47*f*
    efficacy of, 10
    P-Q-R-S-T technique, 131–132
    T-Chart/T-List technique, 164–166, 165*f*
    Word Splash technique, 188–190, 189*f*
brain dumps, 127–128, 138–139
Brain Matters (Wolfe), 10
brainstorming techniques
    Carousel, 81–82
    Exclusion, 89–90, 89*f*
Build a Model technique, 73–77

Camp Songs technique, 78–80
Carousel Brainstorming, 81–82
cause and effect text structure, 15, 15*f*, 55*f*
Charades technique, 83–84

chronological text structure, 13, 13*f*
chunking 20–22, 127, 138–139, 139*f*
Circle (inner/outer) technique, 102–103
Classroom Instruction That Works (Marzano, Pickering, & Pollock), 2–3, 91
compare and contrast text structure, 14, 14*f*, 51*f*
Concrete Spellings technique, 85–86, 85*f*
Cornell Note-Taking System, 166, 166*f*

deductive reasoning, 58
delete-substitute-keep, 174–176
Design a Test technique, 87–88

enumeration text structure, 12, 12*f*
extended summarization techniques. *See* summarization techniques, extended

Frayer Model, 91–93, 91*f*

graphic organizers, 46–56, 47–56*f*, 91–93, 91*f*
Graphic Organizer technique, 46–56, 47–56*f*
groups, summarization techniques for. *See* summarization techniques, oral/interactive

Hammond, W. Dorsey, 190
A Handbook for Classroom Instruction That Works (Marzano, Norford, Paynter, Pickering, & Gaddy), 3
headlines, 28
Human Bingo technique, 94–96, 95*f*
Human Continuum technique, 97–101

individuals, summarization techniques for. *See* summarization techniques, individual
inductive reasoning, 58
initials technique. *See* Acronyms technique
Inner or Outer Circle technique, 102–103
interactive summarization techniques. *See* summarization techniques, oral/interactive

I Read It, But I Don't Get It (Tovani), 10

Jigsaws technique, 104–105
Journals technique, 71, 106–107

kinesthetic summarization techniques. *See* summarization techniques, kinesthetic

Last Word technique, 136–137
Learning Logs technique, 71, 106–107
lectures using summarization, 5
length recommendations for summaries, 25
Lineup technique, 108–112
Luck of the Draw technique, 113

memory, creating long-term, 10
mindfulness, creating, 22–24
mnemonics, 67, 78, 175–176. *See also* Acronyms technique
Model Building technique, 73–77
Moving Summarizations technique, 114–117
Multiple Intelligences in the Classroom (Armstrong), 120
Multiple Intelligences technique, 118–121

note-taking, 166, 166*f*, 170–171, 170*f*

objectivity component in skills acquisition, 24
One-Word Summaries technique, 122–123
oral/interactive summarization techniques. *See* summarization techniques, oral/interactive

paraphrasing, 26–29Partners A and B technique, 127–128
partners techniques. *See also* summarization techniques, oral/interactive
    Circle (inner/outer) technique, 102–103
    Partners A and B, 127–128
    Think-Pair-Share, 173–174
performance summarization techniques. *See* summarization techniques, artistic/performance
P-M-I technique (pluses-minuses-interesting), 124–126, 124*f*
poetry, 80, 85
Point of View technique, 129–130

P-Q-R-S-T technique, 131–132
primacy-recency effect, 3–4
problem-and-solution text structure, 16, 16*f*
puzzle (Jigsaws) technique, 104–105
Pyramid technique, 155–157, 155*f*

RAFT technique, 133–135, 134*f*
reading repetition, 22, 131–132
research, techniques for organizing, 46–56, 53–56*f*

Save the Last Word for Me technique, 136–137
scaffolding, 44
sentence encapsulation, 27
Share One; Get One technique, 138–139, 139*f*
short summarization techniques. *See* summarization techniques, short
Six Thinking Hats (de Bono), 124
Socratic Seminar technique, 97–101, 140–145
Something-Happened-and-Then/Somebody-Wanted-But-So technique, 146–148
songs/singing, 78–80
Sorting Cards technique, 149–150
Spelling Bee de Strange technique, 151–152
spelling techniques
    Concrete, 85–86, 85*f*
    Spelling Bee de Strange, 151–152
    SQ3R, 153–154
spoken summarization techniques. *See* summarization techniques, oral/interactive
SQ3R technique, 153–154
Statues technique, 68–72
summaries, evaluation of, 25, 212–214a
summarization. *See also* specific techniques
    conclusions, 191–192
    efficacy of, 2–6
    importance of, 5–6, 29–30
    rules-based (traditional), 174–176
    steps, 174–176
    techniques chart, 33–38*f*
summarization assignments, unique, 180–184, 182–183*f*
summarization formats, 12–16, 12–16*f*, 25, 51*f*, 55*f*

summarization prompts, 185–187, 186*f*
Summarization Pyramids technique, 155–157, 155*f*
summarization skills acquisition
    analogies use in, 18–19, 65–66*f*
    background knowledge, role in, 9–10
    chunking for, 20–22, 127, 138–139, 139*f*
    evaluation for, 25, 212–214a
    key information identification in, 16–18
    mindfulness techniques, 22–24
    objectivity component, 24
    paraphrasing techniques, 25–29, 215–218a
    priming the brain for, 10
    providing models, 27–28, 174
    text chunking, 20–22, 138–139, 139*f*
    text structure, identifying for, 11–16
summarization techniques, artistic/performance
    Analysis Matrices, 46–56, 51–56*f*
    Blooms Taxonomy Summary Cubes, 60–63, 61–62*f*
    Body Analogies, 18–19, 64–67, 65–66*f*
    Body Sculpture, 68–72
    Build a Model, 73–77
    Camp Songs, 78–80
    Charades, 83–84
    Concrete Spellings, 85–86, 85*f*
    Graphic Organizers, 46–56, 47–56*f*
    Learning Logs/Journals, 71, 106–107
    Multiple Intelligences, 118–121
    Something-Happened-and-Then/ Somebody-Wanted-But-So, 146–148
    Unique Assignments, 180–184, 182–183*f*
summarization techniques, extended
    Analysis Matrices, 46–56, 51–56*f*
    Blooms Taxonomy Summary Cubes, 60–63, 61–62*f*
    Build a Model, 73–77
    Camp Songs, 78–80
    Carousel Brainstorming, 81–82
    Design a Test, 87–88
    Frayer Model, 91–93, 91*f*
    Graphic Organizers, 46–56, 47–56*f*
    Human Bingo, 94–96, 95*f*
    IIuman Continuum, 97–101
    Inner or Outer Circle, 102–103

summarization techniques, extended *(continued)*
    Jigsaws, 104–105
    Learning Logs/Journals, 71, 106–107
    Moving Summarizations, 114–117
    Multiple Intelligences, 118–121
    Point of View, 129–130
    P-Q-R-S-T, 131–132
    RAFT, 133–135, 134*f*
    Rules-Based (traditional), 174–176
    Save the Last Word for Me, 136–137
    Socratic Seminar, 97–101, 140–145
    Spelling Bee de Strange, 151–152
    SQ3R, 153–154
    Synectic Summaries, 160–163, 162*f*
    Taboo, 167–169, 168*f*
    Test Notes, 170–171
    Triads, 177–179
    Unique Assignments, 180–184, 182–183*f*
    Verbs? Change Them!, 175–176, 186*f*
    Word Splash, 188–190, 189*f*
summarization techniques, individual
    3-2-1, 39–40
    Acronyms, 41–43
    Advance Organizers, 44–45
    Analysis Matrices, 46–56, 51–56*f*
    Backwards Summaries, 57–59
    Blooms Taxonomy Summary Cubes, 60–63, 61–62*f*
    Build a Model, 73–77
    Concrete Spellings, 85–86, 85*f*
    Design a Test, 87–88
    Exclusion Brainstorming, 89–90, 89*f*
    Frayer Model, 91–93, 91*f*
    Graphic Organizers, 46–56, 47–56*f*
    Learning Logs/Journals, 71, 106–107
    Luck of the Draw, 113
    Multiple Intelligences, 118–121
    One-Word Summaries, 122–123
    Point of View, 129–130
    P-Q-R-S-T, 131–132
    Pyramids, 155–157, 155*f*
    RAFT, 133–135, 134*f*
    Rules-Based (traditional), 174–176
    Something-Happened-and-Then/ Somebody-Wanted-But-So, 146–148

summarization techniques, individual
(*continued*)
Sorting Cards, 149–150
SQ3R, 153–154
Synectic Summaries, 160–163, 162*f*
Taboo, 167–169, 168*f*
T-Chart/T-List, 153–154, 164–166, 165*f*, 166*f*
Test Notes, 170–171
Triads, 177–179
Unique Assignments, 180–184
Verbs? Change Them!, 175–176, 186*f*
summarization techniques, kinesthetic
Blooms Taxonomy Summary Cubes, 60–63, 61–62*f*
Body Analogies, 18–19, 64–67, 65–66*f*
Body Sculpture, 68–72
Build a Model, 73–77
Camp Songs, 78–80
Carousel Brainstorming, 81–82
Charades, 83–84
Human Bingo, 94–96, 95*f*
Human Continuum, 97–101
Inner or Outer Circle, 102–103
Jigsaws, 104–105
Lineup, 108–112
Moving Summarizations, 114–117
Multiple Intelligences, 118–121
Partners A and B, 127–128
Share One; Get One, 138–139, 139*f*
Socratic Seminar, 97–101, 140–145
Sorting Cards, 149–150
Summary Ball, 158–159
Unique Assignments, 180–184, 182–183*f*
Word Splash, 188–190, 189*f*
summarization techniques, oral/interactive
Body Analogies, 18–19, 64–67, 65–66*f*
Body Sculpture, 68–72
Camp Songs, 78–80
Carousel Brainstorming, 81–82
Charades, 83–84
Human Bingo, 94–96, 95*f*
Human Continuum, 97–101
Inner or Outer Circle, 102–103
Jigsaws, 104–105
Lineup, 108–112

summarization techniques, oral/interactive
(*continued*)
Luck of the Draw, 113
Moving Summarizations, 114–117
Multiple Intelligences, 118–121
Partners A and B, 127–128
P-M-I, 124–126, 124*f*
Point of View, 129–130
Save the Last Word for Me, 136–137
Share One; Get One, 138–139, 139*f*
Socratic seminar, 97–101, 140–145
Spelling Bee de Strange, 151–152
Summary Ball, 158–159
Taboo, 167–169, 168*f*
Think-Pair-Share, 173–174
Triads, 177–179
Unique Assignments, 180–184, 182–183*f*
Word Splash, 188–190, 189*f*
summarization techniques, short
3-2-1, 39–40
Acronyms, 41–43
Advance Organizers, 44–45
Analysis Matrices, 46–56, 51–56*f*
Backwards Summaries, 57–59
Body Analogies, 18–19, 64–67, 65–66*f*
Body Sculpture, 68–72
Carousel Brainstorming, 81–82
Charades, 83–84
Concrete Spellings, 85–86, 85*f*
Exclusion Brainstorming, 89–90, 89*f*
Graphic Organizers, 46–56, 47–56*f*
Lineup, 108–112
Luck of the Draw, 113
Moving Summarizations, 114–117
One-Word Summaries, 122–123
Partners A and B, 127–128
P-M-I, 124–126, 124*f*
Pyramids, 155–157, 155*f*
Share One; Get One, 138–139, 139*f*
Something-Happened-and-Then/ Somebody-Wanted-But-So, 146–148
Sorting Cards, 149–150
Summary Ball, 158–159
Synectic Summaries, 160–163, 162*f*
T-Chart/T-List, 153–154, 164–166, 165*f*, 166*f*

summarization techniques, short *(continued)*
  Think-Pair-Share, 173–174
  Triads, 177–179
  Unique Assignments, 180–184, 182–183*f*
summarization techniques, written
  3-2-1, 39–40
  Acronyms, 41–43
  Advance Organizers, 44–45
  Analysis Matrices, 46–56, 51–56*f*
  Backwards Summaries, 57–59
  Blooms Taxonomy Summary Cubes,
    60–63, 61–62*f*
  Carousel Brainstorming, 81–82
  Design a Test, 87–88
  Exclusion Brainstorming, 89–90, 89*f*
  Frayer Model, 91–93, 91*f*
  Graphic Organizers, 46–56, 47–56*f*
  Learning Logs/Journals, 71, 106–107
  Luck of the Draw, 113
  multiple intelligences, 118–121
  One-Word Summaries, 122–123
  P-M-I, 124–126, 124*f*
  Point of View, 129–130
  P-Q-R-S-T, 131–132
  Pyramids, 155–157, 155*f*
  RAFT, 133–135, 134*f*
  Rules-Based (traditional), 174–176
  Share One; Get One, 138–139, 139*f*
  Something-Happened-and-Then/
    Somebody-Wanted-But-So, 146–148
  SQ3R, 153–154
  synectic summaries, 160–163, 162*f*
  Taboo, 167–169, 168*f*
  T-Chart/T-List, 153–154, 164–166, 165*f*,
    166*f*
  Test Notes, 170–171
  Unique Assignments, 180–184, 182–183*f*
  Verbs? Change Them!, 175–176, 186*f*

summarization techniques, written
(continued)
    Word Splash, 188–190, 189*f*
Summary Ball, the, 158–159
survey, question, read, recite (SQ3R) technique, 153–154
Synectic Summaries technique, 160–163,
  162*f*
synonym generators, 27

Taboo technique, 167–169, 168*f*
"TARGETS" summarization steps, 175–176
T-Chart/T-List technique, 153–154, 164–166,
  165*f*, 166*f*
Test Design technique, 87–88
Test Notes technique, 170–171
text, tools for understanding, 22–24,
  131–132, 136–137, 166, 166*f*
text marking, 22–24, 136–137
text structure, identifying for skills acquisition, 11–17, 12–16*f*, 51*f*
Think-Pair-Share technique, 172–173
3-2-1 technique, 39–40
topic sentences, 17
Triads technique, 177–179

Unique Summarization Assignments,
  180–184, 182–183*f*

Verbs? Change Them! technique, 175–176,
  186*f*
Visual Literacy (Burmark), 18
vocabulary development, 26–27, 188–190,
  189*f*

word banks, 26
Word Splash technique, 189*f*
written summarization techniques. *See* summarization techniques, written

About the Author

Rick Wormeli has taught elementary school and middle school for 24 years and has tutored high school students for 17 of those years. Although he still teaches two weekly math groups and one weekly writing group at the middle school level, he currently spends the majority of his time out of the classroom, writing books and conducting workshops nationally and internationally.

In 1995, Rick was Nationally Board Certified in the first group of teachers to achieve such recognition. He was Disney's Outstanding English Teacher of the Nation for Middle and High Schools in 1996, and he's been a consultant for National Public Radio, *USA Today*, Court TV, and the Smithsonian Institution in Washington, D.C.

Rick is the author of the award-winning *Meet Me in the Middle: Becoming an Accomplished Middle Level Teacher* and *Day One and Beyond: Practical Matters for Middle Level Teachers*. He has a regular column in the National Middle School Association's magazine *Middle Ground*, and he is the featured teacher in the first tape of ASCD's video series, *At Work in the Differentiated Classroom*. Rick can be reached at rwormeli@erols.com.